kadar koli 10

"off the books"

eth press | winter 2016
"kuhdur coly" =
"quotienscumque"

"Patience, Time, Cash, and Strength" (Herman Melville)

kadar koli 10
Copyright © 2016
All rights revert to authors upon publication.
This volume edited by Lisa Ampleman and David Hadbawnik.

Cover images taken in Salmiya, Kuwait, Fall 2015.

Cover design by David Hadbawnik.

eth press
ethpress.com

Inquiries to David Hadbawnik:
dhadbawnik@gmail.com

eth press:
Salmiya, Kuwait
Cincinnati
Toronto
Boston

Contents

Introduction

"Off the Books": not recorded, not taxed. Under the table, stretching the rules.

We conceived of this issue as coinciding with the theme of the 4th Annual Biennial Meeting of the BABEL Working Group (scholars, primarily medievalists, interested in bridging disciplines and testing boundaries) in October 2015. Originally, we planned to feature some work from researchers unable to attend the conference and to have the issue in hand at the conference itself.

Meanwhile, we started considering submissions, and (post another kind of conceiving), guest editor Lisa Ampleman went through the final trimester of her pregnancy and gave birth to a baby. Her son is seven months old as we publish this issue. Additionally, this past summer, editor David Hadbawnik was hired at the American University of Kuwait and moved to the Middle East. For awhile, the journal itself was quite off the books, temporarily postponed.

But those delays in production led to a new richness: in addition to works by creative writers, we feature here several revised presentations from the BABEL conference. We're glad to host these works for people who presented, performed, experienced, and embodied the conference. We see this issue as a bridge between the creative text and creative discussions of text. A few of the pieces here (Mike Rose-Steel, Angela Warner, Tracy Zeman) feature an internal caesura, that white space that allows a place of stillness between sound, as well as the juxtaposition of thought. Across the white space, the medieval looks at the contemporary, the creative at the scholarly. Across the caesura of the page's margin, the text looks at the real. The texts here reflect how we assemble the journal itself. "Still I am linking a word to a word to a word," Ruth Williams says in her prose poem series. We link poem to story to essay, many of which stretch the rules of genre in some way—and which stretch the tendencies of culture. Mike Kelleher notes in his epistolary piece that it's strange he's taking a year to write a letter instead of a quick status message: "It seems so archaic, this idea of writing and sending a letter, what with the easy communication enabled in digital space. But then, who would ever take a year to write an email or a tweet or a Facebook post? A letter is the only form that allows for slow composition (decomposition?)." It took us nearly a year to compose this issue, and now it's able for slow digestion.

And the issue itself is "off the books": though it's available as a print-on-demand document, you may be reading this online or downloaded as a pdf. Online, you can access videos of the performances that Kendra Leonard discusses in her essay. The journal's affiliation with eth press, a division of Punctum Books, means that we embrace its philosophy of providing "radically creative modes of intellectual inquiry and writing across a whimsical para-humanities assemblage" via open-access and print-on-demand services. Paula Billups' piece here, a transcript of a presentation, itself "off the page," describes the process of a communal collage piece. Her statement here acts as microcosm for what we hope *kadar koli 10* does for its writers and their texts: "I intended this as a creative commons. So the book belongs to all of us and to none of us. Because it can't be here unless we *all* do it. The only way *this* book could exist is if all of these people have shown up during these days in this place with this paper. Otherwise it would never have happened."

–Lisa Ampleman, David Hadbawnik

Ruth Williams

KORUS

U.S. Congress Passes FTA with Korea. Experts hailed the U.S. passage of the FTA as a rare bipartisan achievement. Sounds like a song, offered up for a singing. But someone chorused into a canker, a canister loosed in the cannon of commerce. *Amid Tear Gas, South Korea's Parliament Passes FTA With U.S.* We sing a song together, sure, but I wanted to sing one true thing, a sweet opine on this opening. *In addition to strengthening our economic partnership, the KORUS FTA would help to solidify the two countries' long-standing geostrategic alliance.* Yes, an American song is offered up for a singing, true, but, how does a tongue avoid tripping, skipping on foreign soil? Listen. "We sing a song together" skips: *An important decision was made, so history will tell later whether it was right or not. But it will be recorded forever that the Korean Assembly didn't listen to the people.* Thrumming out of commerce, I wanted to say a word that would sing a solo, contribute to a true chorus; but, how to shape the mouth to discord?

On the other side of Seoul some 2,500 protesters clashed with police as they occupied streets and attempted to march at around 9 p.m. I'm not well-suited to speak on foreign soil, true; 한국말—the aspirates and the fricatives—my slab tongue falters. Chords inevitably clash. But someone gives out a sheet and asks everyone to sing, 소소소 (so)(so)(so), I sing along. *Invalidate the FTA Ratification! The Price Will Be Compliance!* My tongue moves, but slithering in its socket, it slips—소 (so) 스 (seu). *The 1% can feed ten thousand!* 소 스, I lisp. *Let's dispose of the KORUS FTA!* 소 스, syllables trip. The next bite is on the baton. *Police used water cannons to disperse them. 19 arrested.* Whose words get taken into custody? Not mine, not mine.

I wanted to be a syllable loosed like a radical register. Smoking out greed and nationalism, a soothsayer, a sly truth-teller. But the song is already being sung. You hear the scales and your tongue grooves right into the rungs. *If you want to know who benefits most from free trade, all you have to do is look at the list of co-chairs steering the U.S.-Korea FTA Business Council: Boeing Company, Chevron, Pfizer, Inc., Goldman Sachs, Citigroup, Inc.* A list of corporate outposts sending out more outposts wherein they sing songs about sending out outposts. Is it any wonder a true word gets garbled, gunked up with greed and nationalism when you trip, dip your tongue into the chorus? My tongue, a knotted clot can only mutter: 송 (Song), 숭(Sung), 승(Seung), never hitting "i" quite right.

Still, I am linking a word to a word to a word. Though there is slippage, as always there is in all words, all ways. *South Korea's foreign ministry was ordered on Friday to make public its correction of errors made in translating the country's English-based free trade agreement with the U.S.* On foreign soil, I slicked my tongue, and knew I wanted to write, not one true thing, but a mistake, a syllable that in slipping would be a warrant.

I don't own the words "greed" or "nationalism." The tongue sloshes syllables around the mouth, tripping like an eel sluicing on to other seas. I'm just singing a song I chorused with others. *Choi called President Lee Myung-bak and the ruling Grand National Party "pro-American to the core," saying he "will not forget Nov. 22, the day when Korean bureaucrats betrayed their country."* Was it a betrayal? Or a national Korean chorus? A true American song? I only know my tongue pushes words, greedy for a new terrain. *The lawyers' association demanded a list of errors for the pact's new 1,300-page version, but the ministry refused, only making a revised copy public.* A note warbles, trilling in the outpost. Please note: there are errors singing in this document.

Tracy Zeman

Solitary Branches & Small Leaves

Barnloft odor of bedstraw & dust
tiny ripples in a system of decay
dogs chase a deer across the field
"land without bottom or edge"
bird with light set against backdrop
unlike *sunrise* or *moonglow*   roving winter-
wren in the weeds   abbreviated tail

High-pitched song   obfuscated reportage
slowly becomes master of everything
that loneliness   a part with power
to suggest a whole   traces of red paint
on the door   attribute high mortality rates
to depravity   to roam to be the by-product
of progress   salt-lick herd of elk or deer

Traps set on headwaters & animal wallows
a sora-rail's black face on gray salt marsh
an otter swimming in the river at dusk
head skimming the water's surface
"loveless & sleepless the sea" I said
"a human problem" I said   "the red flag
is black to the bull" but not to us

*

Some kind of mistake
to buy an empire with beads & cloth
he was scored across both cheeks
face   hands   legs   back
left a tolerably good horse on the shoal
the wave's force determines the pebbles' size
red as rule   starlight fox coralberry

To cut a piece from the soil
of a failed state   panic had seized the men
like wild fire   like fire to cut a piece
from a heart heavily burdened
build bulwark next time   shoreface
lagoon   Little Flat Lick   hills & the new
broken into pieces into self heart bird

Mutable & unfit   so the story goes
to pare down   mountain-mallow
stickseed   pondberry   "species
are unfixed" he said   this greenwashing
once was rock-right   barefoot
& lake & cliffs hanging over
a sea   de-wilded   badger at the center

*

Rain fell intermittently   fiercely
"the dead boy was found clasping a tree"
his wounds had been dressed
with elm bark   no honeyed words
only ill-starred & reduced
turkeys dropt dead off their roosts
hogs frozen to death in their pens

A rope knotted red   ideas of first
& second at odds again
"your love will be safe with me"
I said   red-hearted on the overgrown path
it's important to forget while constructing
a nation   a hybrid space
a man dead in the road left

For some days   failed to recognize new
paradigm   "drunk on the sale
the scale of the natural world"
a gull trying to swallow a starfish whole
a yellow-rumped warbler at Lost Lake
"a woman hid in a hollow
gave birth to a child during the night"

*

No stars yet only frogs croaking
wind in trees   waves in wind
"did not man maim by no" belief
in alterity   delicacy in skin
all else is packhorse & stolen boots
in hard rain & hierarchies
the ocean at night looks like sky

"A grave between the rocks"
a "bodiless campaign" turning soil
to stone   a black gorge   a guidepost
a carapace aglow in darkness
"stayed by the dead hand of inaction"
of star-gazer culler boarder
shipwrecked upon the idea of unwilled

"In the forests maple trees cracked
like pistols & burst open with frozen sap"
I thought of you & where you'd gone
a great destiny   some leave-taking
carried in pieces over the rugged hills
mudholes big-sloughs bare-legged
every few yards some body growing without

Michael Kelleher

Museum Hours

January 2014

Dear Yuko Otomo,

I would like to write a book like your *Study* someday. I picture myself going daily to a museum and selecting a different picture to observe. I take notes, then return home to write poems. I do this every day until I have enough to fill a book. In the process I learn a lot about art.

Which is more or less what I've done while reading *Study*, except that in this case I substituted your book for a real museum. I read a few pages each day, googled images of the art, took notes in the margins. I followed a fairly strict routine through the first section of the book, reading a cycle of poems in the morning and looking at images by the artists later in the day. At night, I reread the poems, using only my memory of the images as a guide.

The routine varied somewhat as I moved through the book. Even though many of the artists were familiar to me, I couldn't recall specific works. Others were totally unfamiliar. I decided to look first and read second or in some cases to switch back and forth between looking and reading. My eyes roamed from the image on my screen to the book on my desk and back.

One night I watched a movie about Ray Johnson after reading your poem about him. It was called, *How to Draw a Bunny*.

February 2014

It's been a month since I started this letter, but I haven't finished it because I keep returning to *Study*, as if to a memory palace, to immerse myself in your experience of art.

The low, mid-winter sun blasts through a large, south-facing window. I have to hold up my left hand to shield my eyes while I read your Robert Frank poems.

Trolley–New Orleans makes me think of the Tennessee Williams' play *A Streetcar Named Desire*. In an archive at the Beinecke Library, where I work, I once found an actual ticket to the actual streetcar named Desire from around the time the play was written. It's a much more interesting artifact than the autographed Playbill it fell out of.

I picture the fluttering curtains in *View from Hotel Window – Butte Montana* to be actually fluttering. In the photo I see that they are still.

***

My first memory of poetry (and painting) has to do with Seurat. When I was growing up I spent Saturday mornings in front of the television watching cartoons. Brief, educational PSAs called *Snippets* sometimes aired between Bugs Bunny and Scooby-Doo. One of them featured Seurat's *A Sunday Afternoon on the Island of La Grande Jatte*.

They filmed the painting from a distance so that you could see the whole picture before they zoomed in to reveal that it had been painted using thousands of individual dots. They used the word Pointillism, and made a point of repeating it.

The *Snippet* ended with a short mnemonic poem intoned by a woman with a British accent:

Seurat
Knew a lot
About dots

***

You mention the date of a Bruce Nauman Exhibition you attended: 4.4.1995. On that date, I was in Quito, Ecuador doing a year of volunteer teaching. A lot of things happened in America while I was there that felt more remote to me than they did to my friends still living in the states. The Republican takeover of congress. The OJ Simpson trial. The Oklahoma City bombing.

On the table in the midst of
a violent incident
flowers in a vase
remain flowers

I watch a video clip of Nauman's *A Violent Incident*. I hear the man say, "You fucking cunt! Don't you ever–" She throws water in his face. She knees him in the balls. The flowers on the table are yellow. Possibly they are tulips or unopened roses. It's hard to tell because the grainy image in the video is of a television on which the video of *A Violent Incident* is playing.

***

Max Beckmann's blacks
like cracks

in the sky you
fall into.

***

I try to figure out which *Untitled* painting by Cy Twombly you are writing about, then realize it doesn't matter.

A massive snowstorm falls outside my window.

***

The verisimilitude of the eyes in Lippo Lippi's paintings establishes a kind of contact across the centuries. I feel like they can see me nearly as clearly as I see them. I wonder if it is Lippi himself staring at me.

***

I am aware of myself sitting at my desk reading. The only light comes through a sliding glass door. Despite the gray winter sky it feels crisp and bright because the ground is covered in snow. I feel compelled to get closer to it. I stand up, holding *Study* in my hand, and walk towards the light. I lean against the glass as I read the rest of the poem I had been reading, *Tracing Time With 2BS and 3BS*.

August 2014

Recently, I saw a movie called *Museum Hours*, by Jem Cohen. It reminded me of everything I loved about your book. It centers on a brief friendship that develops between two solitary people, one a middle-aged Canadian woman, the other a (late) middle-aged Austrian man.

We don't know much about the woman, except that her cousin, who she appears to have met only once, lies in a coma in a Vienna hospital. The woman's phone number was the only one the doctors found in her cousin's possession, so they called her. We see her from behind, standing at a window while talking with someone on the phone. A sibling perhaps. She tells the person on the phone that she must go to Vienna and asks to borrow money. We don't know what the woman does for a living or who this relative is or why she bothers to travel to Vienna to observe the passing of someone she's hardly known.

However, we do learn a bit about the man, mostly through his first-person narration. He works as a security guard at the Kunsthistorisches Museum. He tells us that as a young man he worked security in the music industry and had a lot of fun. We also learn that he is not a passive observer. He pays close attention both to the art he protects and to the people who come to look at it. His observations sound like journal entries read aloud.

The woman, who knows no one in Vienna, comes often to the museum, presumably because she has no money and the museum doesn't charge admission. The guard observes her fumbling with a map of the city. He approaches and asks if he can help. She doesn't know how to get to the hospital where her cousin is dying. He gives her directions and offers to show her around town, even to translate over the phone with the doctor. In one of many asides he tells us that he makes this latter offer in order to verify that she isn't running a scam.

The friendship that grows between them forms the emotional core of the film. We accompany them as they visit the hidden corners of Vienna. We listen in on their conversations as they sit in a cafe. We watch as they dance in a bar. Sometimes they sit together at the bedside of her cousin. The woman likes to sing to her cousin and has a lovely voice.

If the relationship forms the emotional center, the Kunsthistorisches Museum forms the aesthetic and intellectual one. We learn from the guard that the museum houses one of the most impressive collections of Bruegel in the world as well as some choice Rembrandts and Arcimboldos. The director uses works of art to deepen our understanding of the story and its characters. In several scenes the camera cuts back and forth between paintings and carefully composed shots that echo what we see in the paintings without attempting to recreate them.

The guard tells us about the different ways the patrons respond to naked human bodies depicted in art, how the context of the gallery allows them to enjoy erotic feelings without shame. He wryly comments that a lot of the art in the museum is actually pornographic. As he says this, the camera moves from one nude to another, then shifts its view to the various patrons observing these nudes. They are men and women, young and old, skinny and fat.

The camera lingers for enough time on each face that when it returns to the first, we recognize the slender young woman with elongated Renaissance features and dark, straight hair. The camera moves slowly down her naked body, then cuts away. One by one the same patrons we've seen observing these nudes, men and women, old and young, skinny and fat, appear without their clothes. The camera asks us to look at their bodies as they look at the bodies in the paintings. It asks us to feel erotic without shame.

In another scene a docent gives a tour of the Bruegel room to a small group of English-speaking tourists. It lasts almost ten minutes and raises many questions, for instance about the universality and timelessness of art, the tension between the layman's presumed understanding of representational art and his feelings of helplessness, bewilderment, even rage in the face of modern and contemporary art, and also about the ways in which money and class permeate the creation and appreciation of art through the ages.

(In another clever aside, the guard shares with us his memory of a college student who worked with him for a summer, droning on about 'late capitalism.' The guard is impressed with his knowledge, but wonders also if his class consciousness isn't keeping him from understanding some larger truths about art.)

The film spends so much time inside the museum that after a while I could feel the height of the ceilings and I could hear the sound of shoes stepping over the floors and I could see the colors on the walls and the details around the doors and I could imagine standing in the Bruegel room for hours. It began to feel like a place I had visited many times, or a memory of that place.

There is not much else to say about the two main characters. The cousin dies and the friendship comes to its natural end because the woman must return home.

November 2014

(Ars Memoria)

I daydream about making a miniature theater for my daughter. I use an empty shoebox that is at this moment sitting on the floor of the garage as a kind of proscenium. I tear up an old t-shirt to make curtains. I paint a set on the inside and use my daughter's Lego figures for actors. I write a play based on her current favorite book. It's called *Emily's Balloon*. She loves balloons and it so happens her name is Emily. We named her after the poet. The story goes like this:

A little girl's mother buys her a yellow balloon from a street vendor. She lets go. The balloon flies away. She's sad. Her mother buys Emily another balloon and ties it to her finger. They walk home. She lets it go again inside the house and it rises to the ceiling. Her mother ties a small spoon to the end of the string so that the balloon floats just off the ground without flying away. Emily carries the balloon out to the garden. She crowns herself with a garland of flowers. A gust of wind carries the balloon up to a tree, well out of reach. Emily cries. She tells her mother all the things she would have done with the balloon if she still had it. They would have eaten dinner together, brushed their teeth together, gone to bed together. Her mother promises to get it down tomorrow. Emily can't sleep. She looks out her window and sees the yellow balloon still stuck in the limb of the tree. It looks like the moon.

The End.

January 2015

I have been writing this letter for over a year. It keeps getting longer, so that it feels like I might never complete it. Hard to imagine ever sending it. Perhaps I will someday. It seems so archaic, this idea of writing and sending a letter, what with the easy communication enabled in digital space. But then, who would ever take a year to write an email or a tweet or a Facebook post? A letter is the only form that allows for slow composition (decomposition?).

The last thing I wanted to tell you was that I did try to do what I imagined at the beginning of this missive. It was in summer. Several days a week, during my lunch break, I went to the art gallery and strolled around looking for subjects for my poems. The painting I came back to again and again was *Le Café de nuit*, by Vincent Van Gogh. You are probably familiar with it. I'll try to describe it anyway.

As the title suggests, the setting is a cafe at night. The dominant colors are yellow, red, and green, all of them layered on thickly, violently, as if Van Gogh wanted to make you feel nauseous looking at them. At the center is a billiards table on which one red ball and two white balls sit idle beside a single cue laid across its length. Behind the table stands a man in white, the proprietor of the cafe (I read). He's posing, as if for a photo. The white he wears is not really white, it's more of a luminous yellow-green.

All the tabletops and a bar in the background, a door in a backroom seen through a doorway, even a reflection in a mirror are all painted using variations on this color. These contrast starkly with the blood-red walls. Light from four large gas chandeliers struggles against the oppressive darkness of the room. Van Gogh visualizes this struggle with waves of radiating yellow paint that quiver on the verge of extinction. Bottles and glasses litter the tabletops. Five seated patrons, three of whom appear to be sleeping and two in the back, a man and a woman, who may be engaged in a tryst, are the only other people in the frame. A gigantic brown clock reads 12:10.

I returned to this painting on several occasions, paying

attention each time to a different aspect. In my note-book I wrote about the colors, the texture, the composition, the biographical backstory, and anything else I could think of, all with the intention of turning my notes into a poem. The poem never materialized.

On the way to see the Van Gogh one afternoon, I passed a Paul Klee painting called *Joyful Mountain Landscape*. The next morning I wrote a poem in one sitting called *Joyful Mountain Landscape*. Why did this painting lend itself so easily and instantaneously to the writing of a poem while the Van Gogh, which I had looked at and studied so intently, resisted my efforts at poetry? How is it that I have now composed an entire book of ek-phrastic poetry, most of it based on tiny digital reproductions, yet this one painting, which I examined again and again in the flesh, eludes me?

***

(Ars Memoria)

A recording of Louise Bourgeois singing *C'est le mur-mure d l'eau qui chante* and other French children's rhymes. A vacuum cleaner whirring outside my office door. I recall one of her *Couples* sculptures at the Al-bright-Knox Art Gallery in Buffalo. If I mark that spot in my mind, it is easy for me to mentally map the whole museum. I can wander in one direction down a long hall featuring impressionist and post-impressionist paintings (including a work by Seurat) or I can go in another direction through rooms full of pop and op and abstract expressionist art. As I do this I realize that my museum is a kind of memory palace. I could place things on the walls and use them to recall a speech I'd like to give or a list of randomly ordered playing cards. Or I could just wander my own museum, which is built inside of yours.

Thea Tomaini

Folio 135r

He sees a pool of sensuous blue, filled with plump and healthy flowers
The Medievalist shakes the page to see if the water will shimmer.
It is not water, he says.
When he tries to touch it the pool recoils, rippling and bobbing the petals.
It feeds the letters, which grow tall and woody, bold chunks of Gothic
      black block ink.
The letters are familiar, forms almost words, and yet the medievalist cannot
      read their meaning.
His index finger draws emptily down, petting the letters in a plea
      to comply.
Two figures on the page, a man and a woman, hold great woven baskets
      done in the old style.
They harvest the letters with their own bare hands, pulling them up by
      the serifs.
They work around the medievalist's hand, under the palm and between
      the fingers.
The woman smacks him with her home made rake, and he must withdraw
      his hand.
He looks again and the letters are gone, stuffed into the baskets and hauled
      out to market.
One word remains and he sounds it half loud as it's snapped by the stems
      and carried away.

Matt McBride

Two Poems

he perceived a sense of june
following Althea across the yard

as she collected
the well-polished teeth

to her
he seemed
as a living room with a kitchen
and bedrooms built on

the few furnishings were worn and
shabby the carpet threadbare

but there were clean
white curtains on the windows

from the doorway
she could see
a small stocking on the wall

there was no law
against the ivory
in his handkerchief

Althea's breathing
was a series
of gently sloped plains

a flood-borne silt
over the rich frame of Wyoming

Alison Fraser

March-hare

Sullen sunken in drifts and dives, snow in droves
A winter coat to skip for sight, growth and hide the hunter's eye
What I came to know better, March hare running white
    and white
Where it went, afraid to die alone

Let slip and cry little leveret, did you call the winter close
Penning trails in the frozen bog, varying hare, snowshoe rabbit
A hare home range to wander without board
Stealing meat from baited traps

Dogless, let slip fear to bound in eights and circles
It will end before it starts, jugged hare, braced coney,
Seeking winter foods for my plate, a poor ration brought near me
Be near me, lost and remembered, least friend

In the youngest stands the drove waits for striking
In boxing and swerving and stare, an empty cavity long behind
Sighing in the jointed suture when I strike the ground
In silence I see you in late spring snow, hare-coursing

I've never done better than the demon that has fell on me
My prayer over January snow lost and determined
Running on hind and catching boughs
Able not to shake him, covered in lines written in my throat

Raced in rotten snow under the egg moon
Boned me to fraying, water on the latticed ice
Seen through in milky pools my life in Wallace's warren
We watched from the door, drawn in quarters

I was all the time outside, I was everywhere in salt water
On the last single shore, in so small a place, I leave close corners
To rise with hares from the furrows' broken clumps of clay
Coming to my hand mad as the kindness that comes

Greg Allendorf

BOUND IN HUMAN SKIN

this book, pale and tooled. *Palo Santo*
     sifts through the lamplight.

I beat my breast under a bulb, cockeyed
     nipples puffy and insensate, enameled pink.

Were it not for holiness, I'd be a saint.
     My eyes, in their declension,

swab some baroque marvel and move on.
     Interminable curvature, spine

crisp in its hauteur. *Chaleur,*
     les lapins sont en chaleur. The chanticleer

falls backwards from its perch,
     clings and swings, inverted metronome.

I'd imagine somewhere there's a tone
     capable of winning the respect

of an animal. There are bibles
     bound in human skin, for instance;

that seems like something some sweet doe
     would pay to see—a stupid thing like that.

Mike Rose-Steel

The Wittgenstein Vector

Ludwig Wittgenstein's *Tractatus Logico-Philosophicus* (1922) is as famous for its austere and difficult style as for its revolutionary impact on Western philosophy. It consists of a chain of propositions, arranged according to a complex scheme of logical dependence. Each of the seven key propositions propagates sub-propositions, so that instead of a series of arguments, we are presented with the apparent deduction of each entry from its numerical predecessor. Proposition one runs as follows:

1 The world is all that is the case.
1.1 The world is the totality of facts, not of things.
1.11 The world is determined by the facts, and by these being *all* the facts.
1.12 For the totality of facts determines both what is the case, and also all that is not the case.
1.13 The facts in logical space are the world.
1.2 The world divides into facts.
1.21 Any one can either be the case or not be the case, and everything else remain the same.

In later life, Wittgenstein reflected that his minimalist approach had actually left him with a series of 'chapter headings' rather than a full philosophical text; the spaces between the propositions needed to be filled in.

The Wittgenstein Vector has spliced into these imaginary gaps, in place of the anticipated philosophy, a series of poems. Some of these engage directly with the puzzles Wittgenstein was tackling – the possibility of meaning and value, the logic and limits of language – while others give a human, even romantic response to the text's highly controlled and abstract prose. From this mixture of voices and viewpoints new texts proliferate, illuminating or challenging Wittgenstein's writing and its reception.

The Wittgenstein Vector is a project by the *Exegesis* writing collective – Mike Rose-Steel, Jaime Robles, and Suzanne Steele – combining three very different poetic styles and approaches to the base text. Originally a public text-art installation devised by Mike Rose-Steel, it has since evolved into a chapbook, two subsequent exhibition pieces, and a short film, with an expanded publication planned. The installation was constructed on a Victorian brick wall on the University of Exeter Streatham campus. Iron eyes are embedded in the wall, where fruit trees were once espaliered. The laminated poem-cards, with the *Tractatus* proposition on one side and the text on the other, stood at right-angles to the wall, interspersed with art pieces by Jaime Robles, based on Wittgensteinian images and themes. The reader followed the poems using a map provided – according to the numbering system, the poems' themes, individual poets – or at random. The cards bent to the touch and rattled in the wind, adding tactile and auditory elements to the exploration.

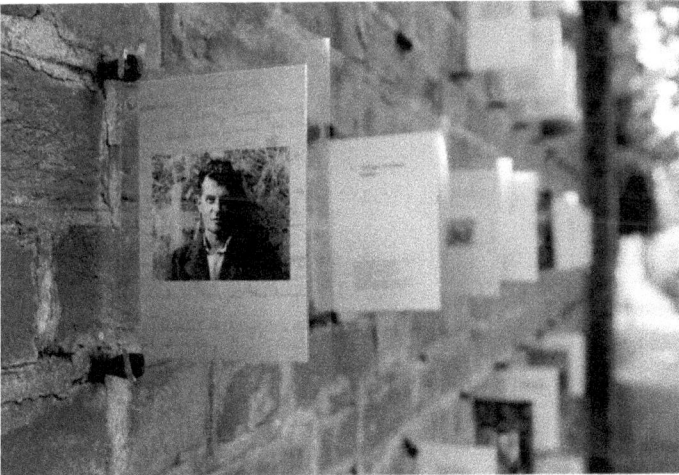

Figure 1 The Wittgenstein Vector, 2012. Portrait of Wittgenstein. Photo Credit Jaime Robles.

Figure 2 The Wittgenstein Vector, 2012. Proposition 7.
Photo Credit Jaime Robles

By dismantling Wittgenstein's book, and allowing new texts and applications to emerge through these fractures, we have in part enacted the philosopher's own later philosophy, with its insistence on the importance of context and use to meaning-making. We also address his discomfort with the idea of publishing an authoritative book of his philosophy, by questioning the finality of any such text. In the preface to *Philosophical Investigations* he says: "I should not like my writing to spare other people the trouble of thinking." We take this to include thinking about how to engage with a text's form as well as its content.

Our explicitly *poetic* engagement with the *Tractatus* has drawn out connections between different elements of Wittgenstein's thought, but also the human and literary contexts of its production. Crucial to all this is the range of possible responses to Proposition 7, the famous closing remark of the book, which Wittgenstein indicated was also the ultimate subject of his philosophical project: "Whereof one cannot speak, thereof one must be silent." In our re-reading and re-writing of his words, we have interrogated this call – for restraint? for despair? – through unexpected modes of speaking and creating.

1.11 The world is determined by the facts, and by these being *all* the facts.

I should very much like to feel *absolutely* safe
as though the world were wrapped in a duvet
muffling the noise of traffic, impossible to disturb.
An infinity of being between fresh sheets.

I would need to be assured that no part, not even
a toe, would protrude from cover into daylight,
that bird noises exist only within
the perimeter of my perception. I could sleep

as cleanly as an algorithm, replicating days,
everything proven true. I would know
that I know the precision of breathing, this world
carved like a yawn, all of one piece.

1.2 The world divides into facts.

The conductor's nod barely disturbs
the brim of his hat – worn to a shine
by years of thumbing down,
donned only for closed rehearsals –
and sends a swoop
more ready than the sea
through the coop of woodwinds,
pearling their hooms and hums
into the new-drummed wave,
until the rushed choir rises,
translated between knife lips
into a flourish of seabirds,
rising
over thundered space and salt.

5. Propositions are truth-functions of elementary
propositions.
  (An elementary proposition is a truth-function of itself.)

In which truth tries on the white coat and arranges itself
(according to the atomic weights of words.)

The mind collides propositions and writes down the patterns.
(The energy of a proposition is its cultural velocity.)

The world takes the form of an answered riddle.
(I have seen the high cliffs around Thebes.)

Mr Wittgenstein writes folk-music, of cherries with no stones.
(*A lover's gift is not a matter of probability.*)

5.47321   [...] Signs that serve *one* purpose are
logically equivalent, and signs that serve *none* are
logically meaningless.

One could imagine a tribe
(let's call them 'us') whose everyday games
had no place for notions of forgiving.
How would this show
in their baking bread, rose beds,
shaking hands, and so forth?
They might instead keep
tallies of Wrongs, carved
on civic columns, or clench
their jaws for a certain length of time
appropriate to forgetting
(by some untroubled mechanism)
Or do we quietly carry
around our necks these things
accumulating
until we no longer sleep
on our stomachs, for fear
of suffocating?

6.1265 Logic can always be conceived to be such that every proposition is its own proof.

You say: "tell me
say *I love you*,"
ladled out
of a church so
in, delving
for poor flashing
into crevices
a thick red
of blood.
(someone
a little self-propelling
the nightlight

you love me,
like a creed
into the ribs
the truth drips
the Onduline heart
darts
and pools:
liquid, a cartoon
This is convincing
of something)
ceremony
of anthrophony.

Paula Billups

Kinesiology of Meaning: Making Pages at the Portable Library of BABEL

Introduction

At the BABEL Biennial Conference 2015 at the University of Toronto, artist Paula Billups presented a weekend-long installation and collaborative project. Assisted by her husband, Scott Billups, and using a hand-built utility cart and a few art supplies, Ms. Billups facilitated a space where conference attendees could use available paper, glue, and ephemera as well as ephemera they brought themselves to create collages which became the pages of a book titled *The Chronicle of the City of Babel* 2015. On Sunday, October 12, Ms. Billups led an hour-long talk and discussion where participants could discuss their experience of the project, titled *The Portable Library of Babel*. The excerpted transcript of the talk is below.

Paula Billups is an artist and writer whose works and curriculum vitae can be found on her websites at www.paulabillups.com and www.dragonfoodpress.com. Her blog is paulabillupsart.blogspot.com and her Facebook page is under Paula Billups Artist as well as Facebook.com/babel.librarian

*

Paula Billups: My name is Paula Billups. I'm an artist and I have a bachelor's degree from the University of Texas in Literature, another from the Lyme Academy of Fine Arts in Connecticut in Painting, and I have an MFA in Creative Practice from the Transart Institute in Berlin. So that's just to say that my history as an artist went from the highly figurative and traditional to the highly conceptual.

When I got the call for proposals for the BABEL Conference, I had never heard of the Conference. I read the CFP and it was such a rich, creative, whimsical, non-stuffy CFP – and so I responded in kind and I wrote a proposal: I'm calling your bluff. And then they accepted it.

(*Laughter*)

And what I proposed was a collaborative process of using ephemera that everybody has brought to create pages. So if you were to come up to the cart you might be bringing ephemera of yours, but there's also the stuff other people brought.

I want to take a few minutes and explain how this came about. In 2013 I was in Venice and I had forgotten my art supplies. I was using placemats and menus and scraps of paper to draw on that were already printed all over, with a sharpie, and I got the notion of crumpling them up. In other words, the paper was already ruined when I got it: I couldn't screw it up. And then I didn't want to treat it as a precious thing and so even with the drawing I would just crunch it up and stick it in my satchel.

And later that year, that led to some large-scale work. I was going around the city of Berlin and pulling down all the rock posters: the city of Berlin is literally covered with paper. If any of you have been there you've seen it. And not only is it everyplace, but it stays there. People don't clean it off, they just leave it. So it gets really weathered and beat up.

I had done painting almost exclusively up until then, so to move into collage was a real shift for me. Part of it had to do with the fact that working figuratively, I insisted on working from life and insisted on working from models, and that's not always possible.

I got deeper into the question of why Berlin has this plethora of paper. I think it has to do with the fact that Berlin is a society that has lived under literally decades of severe oppression: stringent oppression of expression.

My personal thought is, once they got their voice back, they were like, "We're never giving this up again. It's ours now."

You know, so the city is their megaphone, their amplifier, and they're putting their paper up faster than anybody can take it down. If you pull some down they'll be more underneath it –

(Laughter)

– pull *it* down, even *more* underneath. There are light poles in Friedrichshain, these slim silver light poles, but they've been wrapping them with rock posters so long they look like tree trunks –

(Laughter)

Like my dream is to go there with a saw and like cut a chunk out because you can't pull it – like the rings of a tree. And that was the fun part about pulling down paper too, because you know, I was doing it sort of surreptitiously and then I realized that people in Berlin were turning a blind eye, deliberately not noticing. I'd pull it down really fast and stick it in my duffel and get it home. I'd start to pull apart the layers and find amazing things.

And the amazing thing to me was how when you took these images and words out of their context, their original context – which are usually just meant to sell you something – there's a venue or an event or a person or rock star or whatever. And you rip them apart and you recombine them and suddenly there's a different message happening, so questions of context and meaning got really deep for rock-n-roll posters that I ripped off the walls.

I've been almost exclusively working with collage since December of 2013. If you want to ask me later about some series that have happened since then I would love to share that with you.

So I know my paper, I know what I would do to combine these things. I want to know what happens when you give it to – 200 people – and what happens when you have all those voices? I brought a little to seed the project. But I wanted other people to bring their paper and to do this stuff.

The interesting thing about this type of collage is that meaning is highly subjective – what we take away from these symbols and tropes has a lot to do with who we are and where we come from and what we're about. It is really a BABEL idea where the multiplicity of voices and the multiplicity of meanings turns into a highly plastic document. And to the extent that these are the places that we walked through and paper kind of stuck to us as we walked through them – whether I ate at a restaurant, here's a ticket from a museum I went to – bits of us are kind of in this book. So I wanted to know what that book was gonna look like.

I intended this as a creative commons. So the book belongs to all of us and to none of us. Because it can't be here unless we *all* do it. The only way *this* book could exist is if all of these people have shown up during these days in this place with this paper. Otherwise it would never have happened.

So nobody can really take credit but on the other hand we all can, and there's this document now that possibly has a voice, or possibly has a sense to it that maybe none of us intended, but this combination of information is creating that.

So that's the bumper-sticker version of what happens when I think about this project. And what I want to do is talk about your experience in making a page. And the thing I would really love to know, now that we have this book – what do we want to see happen with it? I would like to document the pages individually and post them on the Facebook page and probably my web page, but I wanted to talk to you guys about what's next for this book.

AUD 4: It's interesting the point you make that it belongs to none of us, when I think that what you did sounded like a project in my classroom. I attempted to do the same thing. I already had the pages laid out, like where they're gonna write and where they're gonna put initials and decoration, and then they had to – the instructions were to make somebody else describe it. And we – they lost their minds.

(Laughter)

They lost their minds at the idea that somebody else was gonna touch their thing. And they were like, NOOO No, don't do that, not on my – and so I had to give up the opportunity to think about the fact of communal making, because I think it might have broken them.

(Laughter)

But I find it really interesting the way in which in this moment, we have like people saying this belongs to me and communal making is a thing we don't necessarily understand.

PB: You really have to set up the parameters and the expectations. . . .Yeah, you have to take some managing – it takes self management. You really have to get your ego out of the way.

AUD 4: To give up the ownership of it and communal making is a difficult process in our society. Just thinking about this, and this project: it's a product, it's a community.

AUD5 : I know we do cathedrals or something. You

44

know, it takes generations. But medieval manuscripts: a lot of hands go into it, right? And it's not necessarily documented who they are.

Scott Billups: I am an engineer, so my job is to go into a situation and take the last person's work and create the next level of something. So I'm constantly recycling previous work in order to make the new, best possible work out there. And that's with 100% knowledge that three years from now, someone is gonna come along behind me and do exactly the same thing. I do a lot of hard work anonymously and I am totally fine with that. So people have different takes on the losing of ownership. I'm wondering if where part of that comes from is especially in academia where you have to get your name stapled to your work as a mark of success.

AUD 4: Your work is the analog of communal making and so I think about other times where this might be true. You'll have the same situation where you put your name for a second on this paper, but there's a way in which the knowledge that is produced from this spot is communal. The knowledge itself is supposed to be communal.

AUD 7: I study seventh century cut-and-paste books and books . . . I study a specific archive of these books but also the broader history of cutting these things. And so as I was working with these pages I was kind of thinking about that. And when I went through it here, I was noticing a lot of personal expression that is stripped away in our other scholarly practices. Like we don't see a lot of personal expression in some of our formalized conference papers and yet this kind of peripheral space allows people to say like "I'm a teacher, I get an apple," and put an icon of an apple. So I think it's interesting as an archive of what happens at conferences that doesn't get put into conference proceedings but then gets put back into the book. . .

It's also a lot of hard work. It's fine, but it takes a lot of time. I was just gonna take this thing and merze it a little bit and – it takes time to kind of tear it. Takes time to glue and I'm trying to squeeze it between these sessions and so I'm rushing, and that made me think – you know, that made me think about how that existed. The conference panel that I need to go to where I'm gonna sit and not use my body in any way, that makes me very uncomfortable most of the time, versus standing here and tearing pages. I loved having it here.

AUD 4: It's interesting, the point about the personal part. I might be wrong, but I look at this one over here and I'm like, "Anna!" Anna Wilson who does lots of origami, and it may or may not have been Anna, but immediately reminds me of her humanness other than her academicness.

Michael Collins: So I'd like to speak to that. I really enjoyed the chance to contribute to it. So the culture that I grew up in, I never see represented visually. Or if it is, it's badly done . . . And so I noticed a lot of things I put in with dialect words and phrases that I was really pleased to throw into the chorus. I didn't want them to dominate or stand out; I just really wanted to know they were in there.

The non-prestige dialect – which I can't speak professionally because it would ruin me –

(Laughter)

– it was so neat! As I was working, I got more and more into the idea of home and the culture at home that I can't carry with me into academic spaces even though it's the core of my scholarly practice. And how does that be subterranean and how does this project sort of allow that to come up? So it was really deeply personal, what I ended up doing. But it was satisfying to me, because it became part of this polyglot multicultural multiperspective assemblage, and I was so happy that where I come from was in there.

PB: Right so there's this freedom to put – that's amazing – thank you so much, I'm so glad. What I hear is that this creates a relatively safe space to reach for things that you may not otherwise be in a position to engage, and it may be that the multiplicity of voices kind of helps that. . . .This question of the hidden thing is something that I think is worth talking about.

AUD 3: One thing that happened as I was doing mine – at first it was playing, but the more stuff you pick up, I find myself saying, "Oh, this reminds me of this!" Or I suddenly have this personal association with this. So it went from being, "Oh, this is a fun thing" to "This is something actually personal that reminds me of . . ." So that moment of transition was interesting to me.

AUD 5: It's so interesting – how personal it can get when you are using things that aren't yours. You are using these things from scratch, you're appropriating.

PB: That transformation is a wonderful explorative process because these things when they are unhitched from their original meaning can be quite surreal. You know, you see a woman in Elizabethan dress and a person spitting fire and a 1910 automobile and then you see a fish. And these things were obviously meant to communicate certain things before, but now you just have these bits, and what does an Elizabethan woman and a fire-spitting man have to do with a fish and a car?

It occurs to me that there's a process of letting go. . . . and some of those things are hard to give up. There was a woman who brought a note she'd been anonymously sent that she wanted to incorporate. She said she had a hard time letting it go, and then when this project came up, she was like, "I know what I'm gonna do with this."

And you know, trying to bring things from home. I brought a yearbook from 1966, my uncle's high school from Amarillo, Texas. . . . Michael read the book: he read just a little inscription that someone had written my uncle, who passed away about 20 years ago. And all of a sudden I was like, "Someone said something really beautiful and sweet to my uncle, and I'm hearing that message now forty years later." And it just felt like this overwhelming sense that he was suddenly there.

And so he was like, "Maybe you wanna hang on to this?" And so we took out the pages that we knew were directly associated with my uncle, and then the yearbook goes back in.

AUD 6: When we look at it, it looks like a collage and it obviously is very meaningful to that particular person. But to a reader who doesn't have necessarily have the same background it doesn't necessarily have the same meaning. I'm wondering, like were there explanatory pieces that went with them?

MC: My annotations, I don't know if they make sense to someone embedded in the culture I grew up in

(Laughter)

but like . . . I wrote "streelish hand" in my schoolboy cursive, underneath a student feedback comment that had been submitted that wasn't mine. But it was also written in a cursive hand. And "streelish" is an adjective that basically means "slovenly," like untidy in a way that shows a lack of care and perhaps relating to a lack of moral character. I meant there to be a comparison between that handwriting and my hand, and I was implicating myself as being streelish. And I mean in a way it reflected back on my pedagogy. When I'm a good teacher and a bad teacher it comes from the same point of my character, in that I'm a very enthu-

48

siastic and emotive character . . . who does not do a lot of planning, and who is not very organized in his method.

PB: I'll reflect on two series of collages I've done in the past year that were about some deeply personal experiences. And I knew, as you were saying, that that was such a personal narrative and our visual associations with things are pre-verbal. They're sub-level. And things hit us. They get past our cognitive processes, sneak through the wires and grab hold of your heart. So there's this hide-and-seek going on.

In other words, it's possible to bring something deeply personal to the pages and also find ways to stay hidden in ways that may be important.

SB: I remember you saying part of the origin of the series in Berlin, and how these are histories revealing itself in the culture, and there's two aspects of that. You mention the idea that "We've been shut up for so long, we're going to express everything very loudly and you can't stop us any more." But there's also "We never had privacy before and so we're gonna put out symbols without necessarily telling you what they mean." So there's these levels of exposed and hidden.

PB: Well, and there's this interstitial space that as an artist I occupied without realizing it. I prefer ephemera because that ephemera was meant for public consumption. So my fascination with that paper, particularly in Berlin, was that. To ask Berliners, "What was your experience?" – that's not appropriate. But I can read something about the city through its paper. But I am only allowed to read what they show.

Emmanuel Levinas considered the possibility that we need to have that kernel of totally private space, and that's super important not to encroach on. And this is anathema to a culture where we are oversharing and kind of digging and using all of this. . . Understanding that ephemera, as it appears in our lives, is full of meaning. You know, a designer put together a rock

poster with a fire-breathing fish –

(*Laughter*)

– they had a reason they did that, but they are not letting anything out the gate that they did not intend to let out the gate. And I am still able to interact with them in this kind of cooperative way.

AUD 4: I love that it's in a book form too, because I feel like a book is a thing that has dislocated that: kind of a negotiation of public and private. . . The page is not a transparent space for meaning, where meaning has to be made by the person who decides to take the act of actually unfolding it and looking a this collision of two pages.

So how would this be different if it were just a project of a set of collages? I feel like it would be totally different. Maybe not less meaningful, depending on the space, but I just love the use of the book.

PB: So there's even a kinesiology of meaning.

AUD 4: Each page has these surprising moments and juxtapositions, but also where the pages end up.

PB: There's this desire on my part, because this is a collaborative work, to have a very light fingerprint. But at the same time, I am bringing ephemera. I am present when people are asking "how do I do this?"

And I don't have a sense of sequence . . . but it's gotta be put together in some kind of sequence, otherwise they're just – all over the floor.

(*Laughter*)

So that is going to affect the read. And it matters – it totally matters. You resequence the pages, and get a totally different sent of meanings. I am having an effect on how this gets understood.

AUD 4: I like how tangible it is, going back to the fact that it's a book. It's something that you don't just look at, but you're actually interacting with it and the hands going into it.. . . There's this collective process of discovery, but it's sort of in the air. And a conference is like that too. So it's not just the paper that's been prepared and how they're presenting, but what order they're in, who else is in the room: the sense of collective. And the book makes it something you can see and touch and move between.

PB: So is it something that we should allow to travel, should it go other places, could it be exhibited in other forms, should it stay on my shelf? should it stay with Eileen? . . . It would be wonderful to have it be in a sort of library form, wherever it's staying. If it's staying at my house and someone says, "I have a conference I want to bring it, to talk about it," . . . it has a way of traveling back and forth.

MC: I really hope it gets digitized! I'd really like a chance to look through these after I've had a refractory period to gather my thoughts and my energy and at leisure to do it because it's a big thing and it takes time to go through.

PB: If you are one of the people who made a page, did it make a difference to have other examples, did it help? Or did you not use that?

MC: I didn't really use the other pages as a model myself. Serendipity is such a big part of this. . . like these three things and I come across something that sparks an idea in my head. . . I was just interested in seeing what happens when I started bumping against the material.

PB: If you worked on it, what worked, and what could be better? And if you are thinking about working on it, what concerns do you have, and what questions do you have in your mind?

AUD 9: I loved the collaborative experience of it, I loved the nature of what other people were working on at the same time. . . the conversation you have about this stuff informing what you create, and becomes more pieces of the page.

MC: I also wish I'd brought – anything – 'cause everything I used was found and none of it was raw meaning, but I was really – I find these resonant things that were useful. So I ended up finding the direction it took us. These fragments of home which is a really comforting kind of thing. But I love the idea of this traveling around the world and things that I put in there having that for someone else, leaving these little seeds for future people to harvest, you have no idea! But in terms of my own experience making a page, it was great.

PB: So we're at the end of our session, so we're gonna fold this thing up and get it back out in the hall so people can keep making pages – thank you guys so much for being part of this.

Applause.

Angela Warner

Colliding Identities: The Intertextuality of Women's Work

I hadn't at all planned on going to the 2015 Babel Conference here at the University of Toronto. I was already despondent from not having anyone to watch my kids, meaning I had to miss all of Friday's sessions, and I didn't think I could afford, work-wise, to go on the Saturday or the Sunday. But after seeing everyone's tweets about all of Friday's sessions, I felt pulled to join in. So the next day, Saturday, I pretended really hard that I could shift my academic work day to Sunday so that I could attend sessions. I felt so guilty not focusing on my work, and yet shirking my duties with respect to one type of work led to a wholly different kind of work that was just as, if not more, important in its own way.

After the midday plenary, there was a poetry session centred around participants creating pseudo-translations of medieval texts. In this session, there was a woman, Vanessa Scott, wearing a scarf made of crocheted chain links; she was carrying around yarn and crochet hooks for this scarf-as-art piece, the purpose of which was to representationally link women with textiles/textuality and teaching. Anyone who was able to could contribute a crocheted link or two to the chain, and if they weren't able to, they could be taught. I already knew how to crochet, so I decided to give it a go and began crocheting there in the translation session between writing pseudo-translation poems. When I delivered my completed links to Vanessa after the session, she gave me several lengths of yarn to work on as the day wore on, telling me, "You're good at this. I want to see no less than 9!" Sort of wide-eyed and a little disoriented at the thought of being good at crochet and now being asked to fulfill an unexpected request using that skill, I took her up on the offer and crocheted during the unsession dance performances of Cleopatra, Philomela, Salomé that followed. I then brought the yarn with me to the next session, one on Hybrid Pedagogy, and I worked steadily there, snapping and tweeting these photos, calling them Women's Work and Multitasking.

As a single parent of two kids — a title that feels both foreign and familiar, and a new-to-me role I'm getting used to as days pass — and as an older student, I've had to face a work-life balance that men do not have to face: the daily multitasking and emotional labour of being a female-bodied, feminine embodied person in this world. I am coming to terms with my own internalized misogyny. I have oft referred to myself as a gender-neutral "parent" rather than as a "mother" because of the baggage contained in the word "mother." I call myself a person, rather than a woman, because of how uncomfortable I feel being called and referred to as a woman. To be clear, I don't identify as gender-queer or transgender; I identify as female, but identifying *as* a woman and *as* a mother has felt problematic for me, in part because, in my understanding of how this world works, women are seen as less-than. Society has taught me that *people* are important, but *women* are less so. And so I am a parent. I am a person. But on Saturday, all of that shifted.

A poem I wrote in Saturday's poetry session, a pseudo-translation based on an Old English text, reflects the tension I feel between the staccato relationship with my mother and my nigh-resplendent experiences as a mother to my kids, as I work to give them so much more maternal connection than I experienced as a daughter to my mother.

Crocheting while writing poetry is a familiar place for me. I have found myself in that same space often in my own home. I am a poet. I knit. I crochet. However, crocheting in the Hybrid Pedagogy session, I felt really uncomfortable not paying what looked like full attention to the speakers in the discussion. I felt like I wasn't playing the game properly. It was a collision of my identities, a collision of worlds — of the private, home-based sphere of textual craft and textile-based creativity, and of the semi-public, professional sphere of academia. While sitting with that discomfort, I realized that I was also there in that session as a visible performer of women's work, clearly demonstrating that I could multitask and pay attention just fine to what was being said. After all, this is what Stitch'n'Bitch groups and sewing bees are all about — talking and connecting while creating textile-based crafts. I felt on showcase in that session as a woman doing what is traditionally women's work in a [traditionally male-dominated] academic and very technological setting: people were live-tweeting, and the session was centred around digital publishing and hybrid pedagogy. It wouldn't have had the same effect were a man crocheting in that session. It would *look* like the same action, but it would not *be* the same action for the simple and laden reason that crocheting is an activity centred in the female sphere. A man crocheting seems transgressive because it's less typical, and yet, a woman crocheting in an academic setting, in its own way, is far more transgressive, blurring the lines between what comprises women's work and what is "work appropriate" for a woman. It felt subversive and rebellious, sitting there with hook and yarn, feeling exposed but unapologetic, crocheting in a room full of academics, and it reminds me of my assertion that for me to stay at home with my children for several years was a feminist choice because I was the one making that decision. Believing such a thing blurs the lines we've collectively drawn in the sand about a woman's capacity to make decisions about how she self-defines, who she is capable of being, and where she is allowed to be all of who she is. If I could bring feminism into the stay-at-home parenting gig, I could certainly bring my crocheting self into the academic setting.

I incorporated the textiles and the digital medium in a tweet, which brought the chain full circle, visually linking women's work and multitasking to academia and the digital world of connected and interconnected social media.

Because this particular session was structured as a discussion from the outset, with no papers or presentations, I was able to participate, which is new for me. In a discussion thread, one of the organizers had suggested that it was the *labour* of an article or of the editing of an article that was important and not the process of it. Struck with simultaneous visions of laboring through the process of birthing my children and laboring through the process of writing, I raised my hand between crocheting chain stitches and said, initially, "You cannot extricate labour from process." He nodded, in a dawning accordance. I finished what I had to say and then tweeted this quote, which the other organizer immediately retweeted. We were all multitasking and connecting, both in person and on Twitter. Yet, I had the extra with me. The crocheting. The additionally-visible layer of multitasking as a woman in this world, labouring and processing, stitch by stitch, tweet by retweet, connecting with others in that room, others on Twitter, connecting with all the other women crocheting and dancing and sharing other parts of themselves, and finally, connecting with other aspects of myself that I didn't know were there. Something clicked for me over the course of that day, and the connection I felt there in that session, a connection that had been building for who knows how long but which was brought forth as a result of my saying *yes* to the part of me who crocheted coupled with the self-conscious discomfort I felt in this visible collision of my identities, manifestly working on "women's work" in an academic ("male") setting … this connection reached me in a deeply internal place, allowing me to truly experience myself as the multifaceted person I actually am:

Connection. Women's work. Labour. Process. Motherhood. Multitasking. Poetry. Academia. Texts/textiles/textuality and the inter-connected inter-textuality of Womanness.

I am not just an academic. I am not just a poet.

I am not just a parent; I'm not just a person.

Because of the experiences that day, I feel safe now to say I am a *mother*. I feel empowered now to say I am a *woman*.

It was in the multifaceted process of connection that I finally felt *woman* to be *more-than* instead of *less-than*. And with that connection, a sense of absolute pride washed over me. I am a woman. I am a woman. I had finally joined, not just in name but in spirit, too, all the women before me and all the women around me, as a woman, a link that carried with it all of our collective experiences.

Because of the structure of this conference, the way it blurred lines of what is expected, the way it pushed boundaries creatively and with the utmost respect, the way it allowed participants to exhibit and experience fuller expressions of themselves through poetry, art, dance, crochet, the way it broke down barriers between audience and presenters, between the multiple identities we each have as individuals, and very largely because of the session centered on women's arts of the body and the series of related unsessions (the crocheting unsession being one of them) for which I would very much like to thank Irina Dumitrescu and Vanessa Scott, a safe environment was established for people to create and to express facets of themselves that usually get left behind at academic conferences, to weave them into the academic setting creating a collective intertextuality. Even in reading the Code of Conduct at the beginning of the program wherein are listed "Ombudsmaidens: Eileen Joy, Myra Seaman, Suzanne Conklin Akbari", I felt like women had my back. Not just these marvelous Ombusdmaidens, and the efforts they took to create a safe and consciously respectful space for everyone there, but Irina and Vanessa for collaborating on the crochet unsession, Irina especially for putting together the series of un/sessions, and all the other women at the conference who put themselves out there as the brilliant, creative, thoughtful multifaceted women they are. It wasn't just one aspect of this conference or another – it was all of it and the ways these women joined together to share aspects of who they are.

By bringing women more centre-stage, by deliberately incorporating into an academic setting these varied expressions of womanhood, giving them due acknowledgment, I was able to be a truer expression of myself, further connecting the parts of myself that typically get denied any airtime in an academic setting. Furthermore and most importantly, I was able to get in touch with self-identities that I'd long held at bay. I no longer balk at the word "mother"; I identify with it. I no longer balk at being called a woman. I very much am one, and I finally feel it to be true. The half a day spent at this conference was an extremely unifying experience for me, one that helped heal parts of myself I had no way of knowing how to tend to otherwise.

Anglo-Saxon Riddle 47
Moððe word fræt--   me þæt þuhte
wrætlicu wyrd   þa ic þæt wundor gefrægn,
þæt se wyrm forswealg   wera gied sumes,
þeof in þystro,   þrymfæstne cwide
ond þæs strangan staþol.   Stælgiest ne wæs
wihte þy gleawra   þe he þam wordum swealg.

Mother poem
Mother words free me   thoughts thought
wringing words that I wonder   that greening
that forswearing, worming its way,
     undergirding the sum of who we are and were
this theology   thrumming fast   a quickening
this strange staple   strangling what never was
while gleaning   these words that swear…

Jonathan Basile

(Re)creating Borges' Library of Babel

libraryofbabel.info is a digital archive of every possible permutation of a page of lower-case letters and basic punctuation, modeled after the universal library described by Borges in "The Library of Babel." It has received some attention from the press, who tend to frame its existence as though technology has now made possible the reality of something that was previously only a fantasy. For example, the following appeared in a Slate article entitled, "Jorge Luis Borges' 'Library of Babel' Is Now a Real Website. Borges Would Be Alarmed": "But still: Borges intended his story to be ironic – haunting because it was impossible – so he would surely be alarmed to know we've moved a bit closer to its realization."[1] I prefer to emphasize a different reading of these two virtual archives – mine and that of Borges – that does not conform to popular notions of technological progress. Indeed, we tend to represent the future itself as the advent of technological change, associating the past with nature, and similarly relate the advance of rationalistic science to the displacement of mytho-poetic thought. The universal library, in all the forms it has taken throughout history, offers a reminder of the shared origin of technology and art in a τεχνη that, if not a unified essence, is at least their common rupture or deconstructability.

In an essay written two years before "The Library of Babel," entitled "The Total Library," Borges ties the origin of the universal library to the thought of the

---

1) Waldman, Katy. "Jorge Luis Borges' "Library of Babel" Is Now a Real Website. Borges Would Be Alarmed." *Slate*. N.p., 30 Apr. 2015. Web. 25 Oct. 2015. <http://www.slate.com/blogs/brow-beat/2015/04/30/jonathan_basile_brings_borges_library_of_babel_to_life_with_an_eerie_gibberish.html>.

Ancient Greek atomists. He traces a lineage of authors who recognized that language could be considered as a purely combinatoric process, from German proto-science fiction author Kurd Lasswitz and Lewis Carroll back to Cicero and Democritus. The latter, as reported by Aristotle, compared the possibility of the complexity of experience emerging from the permutations of basic atoms to the possibility that the complexity of language could emerge from the permutation of its basic elements, the letters.

I prefer to think of the online library as an extension of this tradition whose provenance is mythical and poetic, rather than as a technological novelty. Indeed, the most common conclusions drawn from its existence – that everything has been written so we can now only repeat, that language is possible without our intentions toward meaning – have always been true of language. These principles stem from the iterability that belongs to the essence of language; in order to function as signs, all marks must be recognizable in diverse situations, and thus always remain, "separable from their internal and external context and also from themselves, inasmuch as the very iterability which constituted their identity does not permit them ever to be a unity that is identical to itself."[2] That is, the spoken or written word will be possible in the absence of its sender, receiver, and other contextual markings, and something like repetition will haunt it at its origin. So, language did not become repetition upon the creation of libraryofbabel.info. Iterability belongs to the essence of language, which means that it is older than any human thought or action, in fact older than history and temporality themselves.

The roles played by visitors to the website also have their precedents. The most common responses of users are 1) Can we begin to mark off "meaningless" pages

2) Derrida, Jacques. "Signature, Event, Context." *Limited Inc.* Baltimore: Johns Hopkins UP, 1977. 10. Print.

so that ultimately we will find the meaningful ones? and 2) Can we design another computer program to search through the library and find the pages we desire? (The library is already searchable, but one can find only the exact words one searches for – what these users want is to find what they don't know how to look for.) Anyone who remembers Borges' story will recognize that these responses correlate exactly to the sects formed by the librarians of Babel, who feud over the proper way to seek the library's truly divine texts. The Purifiers try to destroy books that contain nothing they recognize as meaningful, while others seek the Man of the Book, who would have found and read the master catalogue of the library. We can see again in this instance that there is no novelty to the digital instantiation of this project, but rather that its users fall into the archetypal roles already foreseen or created by the fiction. If anything, libraryofbabel.info does not make fiction real, but rather submerges users in its fictional precursors.

What is an archive, if this collection of every possible permutation of text pre-exists all its instantiations? Can an archive exist with no substrate, embedded in the essence of language? Consider the most important discovery of Borges' librarians, the book that reveals to them that their universe contains every possible permutation of text. Its contents are described as "the rudiments of combinatory analysis, illustrated with examples of endlessly repeating variations."[3] This can only be a sly joke from Borges, who knows well that every book in the library, and every book ever written, can be viewed as an example of combinatorics. The archive of the divinely created word is coterminous with the archive of examples of mechanical repetition – both are latent possibilities of every set of signs, and this always hauntingly present archive is awakened by a thought, without requiring or creating any change in the material world. An archive can be virtual, not merely in the online, digital sense of libraryofbabel.

3) Borges, Jorge Luis. "The Library of Babel." *Collected Fictions.* Trans. Andrew Hurley. New York, NY, U.S.A.: Viking, 1998. 114. Print.

info, but in the sense that it has no material presence whatsoever, belonging instead to the essence of language or thought.

Everything we have considered thus far could be gathered under the heading of the deconstruction of invention and discovery. Every act of supposed invention must constitute itself in fundamentally iterable elements, making it indistinguishable from a discovery or finding of what already was. Thus, the inventor is a bricoleur. As Derrida describes it, "Whereas the act of invention can take place only once, the invented artifact must be essentially repeatable, transmissible, and transposable. Therefore, the 'one time' or the 'a first time' of the act of invention finds itself divided or multiplied in itself, in order to have given rise and put in place an iterability."[4] It is just as true that every act of discovery, the encounter of what was latent, unrecognized or unrecognizable, forgotten or unforeseen in whatever was there already, partakes of invention, requires an active interpretation and translation of some inheritance. There is discovery in invention, and invention in discovery. Perhaps we can recognize some of this difference or novelty in the different uses found for the library now that it exists online. While Borges' librarians were most interested in seeking religious truth, and typically reported only findings of surrealistic accidental poetry ("*Combed Thunder*" or "*The Plaster Cramp*"), visitors to libraryofbabel.info are just as likely to use it to create ASCII art or look up internet memes. None of this was impossible in Borges' library, and of course it retains the status of a repetition; still, it should keep us mindful of what may, without any mark to secure its certainty, merit the names of difference, novelty, or invention, if there is any.

4) Derrida, Jacques. "Psyche: Invention of the Other." Ed. Elizabeth Rottenberg. *Psyche: Inventions of the Other.* Ed. Peggy Kamuf. Trans. Catherine Porter. Vol. 1. Stanford, CA: Stanford UP, 2007. 34. Print.

Works Consulted

Borges, Jorge Luis. "La Biblioteca De Babel." *Obras Completas*. Buenos Aires: Emecé, 1974. 465-71. Print.

Borges, Jorge Luis. "La Biblioteca Total." *Ficcionario: Una Antología De Sus Textos*. Ed. Emir Rodríguez Monegal. Mexico, D. F.: Fondo De Cultura Económica, 1985. 126-28. Print.

Borges, Jorge Luis. "The Total Library." *The Total Library: Non-fiction 1922-1986*. Trans. Eliot Weinberger. London: Penguin, 1999. 214-16. Print.

Eileen G'Sell

WOMEN & CHILDREN

This world is filled with women and children. They are lifting, spitting. They are blocking the sun. They are dirtier than you ever remembered—holier, too. Done up, gone out. When one of them heads to the front of the line, the equator twists into taffy. Low-level clouds play tricks on rain; mountains sweet-talk snow.

There were boats we used to put them in. They had years to drift so far, so good. They had ways with words, with wind, with flame. We warmed our mouths with impossible love. But when time arrived to take them back, no one knew what to talk about. Like the sound of a soda can opened

in space, their song released and detained our ears. What more could the good world offer us? What else would we ever truly deserve? Maybe the reason the moon moves on is only because we notice it. On quiet horses the women and children are storming the city today.

ODE TO CALIFORNIA CHROME

I started, and I got my start.
Strangers watched, or cried,
made bets, and did not
seem so strange to me.

I was given a bracelet
from a gift shop in Chicago, I won
admission to a hill of trees, went blonde,
bought a house, sang songs to my dog
while sweeping the stairs of his good dog fur.

O, effort, O glory, O old desperation,
O anything sweaty and foaming at the mouth,

defeat is bitterest to those
whom victory sweetly
clouded once, or twice.

I do not believe in God, or anyone
to whom I'd owe my afterlife.
But I say, sweet steed, track to track,
you are no golden ruin.
Everyone wanted

to see you fly, and wanting
something that badly only made you
more like everybody else;

as anything worth believing
in, every belief the run made bright
bursts back to a day so dirty
every one of us swallowed

our fears and said, "This
is the first thing
we ever expected. This
is the end." And we race on.

EXPLICIT

The nice thing was, we were in love, with enough sparkling water to last a week's end. Songs once filled with shadow shared the sound of vagrant summer, the one where my legs looked better than ever and Gwen Stefani lauded my shades. That really happened. And so must we. And so must Eva Longoria ads at the bus stops of Barcelona. And so must God and the absence of God and Sagrada Família never complete. I am sorry I say "Fuck you!' sometimes when I mean it as a compliment. It is true that my feet are never ever clean. My Buddhist friend named Rachel says I'd make the greatest get-away driver. I buy a MINI Cooper from an artist from Korea. I drive it fast while singing slow. Take the "o" out of poet and you have a little pet. Tack a "b" onto "itch" and your skin calms down. When I stray, eat the "r" with your finest silver. When I slide, sip the "l" in a crystal flute, then discern which one to land on.

Les Kay

Instead of Freezing by Fear

The difficulty of her position was not made clear to Monsieur B_____ until the details of their Arrangement had been settled and he had no way of extricating himself from the situation short of Divine Intervention. Consequently, after the true nature of her condition was revealed by a sudden tendency to spend an inordinate portion of the morning in the water closet, he ensured that his affairs were in order and called for the coachman, who loaded their trunks with nary a whisper, knowing full well that the slightest intimation of understanding might result in M. B_____ opting to request the termination of his services.

Shortly after midnight, the manor on Rue d'_____, which M. B_____ had fancied his own harbinger of heaven's biding delights before he realized her maidenhead had not been his to take, receded into the snow-covered streets as phantoms dissipate from the mind's ruminations when the final carafe of brandy is at last empty.

On the outskirts of Paris, as the carriage rattled south down the Seine toward the river's source in D_____, M. B_____ could hold his tongue no longer. He turned to his young bride, who held her belly as if the coach's continued jostling might disturb the delicate balance between decorum and the evening's earlier repast, and asked, without the semblance of a prefatory gesture, the name of his previously unperceived rival.

Rather than turning to her new household's head in conscientious genuflection or erecting a veritable fortress of further deceit—as M. B_____ expected— she looked, quietly as falling snow, out the carriage window as if an adequate answer could be found in the half-frozen contours of the Seine, as if he had, rather than posing a question of such magnitude, suggested the journey still before them was long, that she would need her rest, that their excursion was necessitated by nothing more than a whim that the new mistress of the household become acquainted with their estate in D_____ as he would have his associates in Paris believe. The subsequent image of her serenity—the curls of her auburn hair faintly reflecting the starlight as her head eased against the doorframe, and her eyelids, just visible in the oppressive darkness of the cabin, fluttered with the first signs of long deferred sleep—left him furious as a shepherd who wakes from an unintended repose only to find his flock absent a prized sheep. Nonetheless, M. B_____ could not find it in himself to disturb her, so he let the flourishes of his imagination cascade through a series of machinations with the sole purpose of cleansing the unsightly blemish he believed had marred the hitherto unsullied state of his honor: he considered how he could, upon discerning the man's name, track the scoundrel across the countryside of France, offer the vagrant a choice of weapons with his tight-lipped coachman as his second, and at last dispense the doubtless brigand of his nettlesome ways, and he witnessed his own precarious visions of the original slight, unable to prevent himself from picturing the field-rough hands of some highwayman pilfering his betrothed's innocence, which should rightfully have been his, and he let himself, alas, consider the conjecture, remote as it may have been, that his unknown nemesis might have acted in sinful concert with the woman sleeping beside him, and all the while the snow did fall, constant in its circling, swirling around the rumbling coach in what seemed to him an emblem of what might have been until, at last, he slipped into sleep's figments of crimson ice, crushed beneath footsteps in fields he'd never seen.

As the sun slipped above the now snowless fields on the outskirts of T_____, she woke M. B_____ with the slightest of brushes of her magpie-sized hand, and without the prevarication one might expect from a woman of her age and station, Madame B_____ asked, forceful as an axe lodged in frozen firewood, "What need have I of his name now that we have yours?"

Careful Wishing

The difference is spreading.
– Gertrude Stein

When the final buttress was bolted onto the city, the final applicants for residency screened, and the city wrapped in its eventual mist, we, at last, had no need of Steinbeck, Stendahl, or Stein Mart. We spread Van Goghs and Picassos across children's playpens. Michelangelo and Giacometti became nothing more than descriptions of popular coat racks. Our automobiles were reassembled into swing sets and jungle gyms. The star machine was dismantled in favor of municipal issues. Fabergé eggs, diamonds, and platinum were hung from former Christmas trees in dark alleys to light the footsteps of women and men walking home from their day's duties. We fed what caviar remained to mousers and other communal pets, truffles were fed to the petting zoo pigs, and all saffron was used to make rice for the first Forgetting Day feast.

All progressed according to plan. The citizens filled the stadium to watch our children play hopscotch and skip rope in turn. The denizens of our fair city beyond the mist enjoyed the weekly forgetting so much, another day was added unanimously to the week for yet more forgetting. Everyone became mayor for a week, everyone taught the children for a week, and so our duties were divided among us. Flowers bloomed from every window. The music of chatting and occasional embraces filled the streets as need be. No one thought of before, except to teach the children what might happen if they breached the mist.

Sooner than anticipated, our language changed. Embroidered shirts were left on curbsides. Business cards shredded for confetti. Bylines vanished from the minutes of each mayoral meeting. Vows were left like lilacs in the central square. Terms like *I*, *my*, and *theft* were struck from the shrinking habitat of the dictionary.

Our history was forever present as nothing more than fog.

Then, after more years than could easily be counted, one of the first, who had been nothing more than a child when the rest of the world vanished from view, woke on the week before his mayoral term to an image of an elderly woman's face half-obscured by white petals falling from what seemed a familiar tree. Against custom, he sat away from us during lunch, contemplating the floating images as he sipped at his tea and nibbled at bits of hummus. Despite such an anomaly, that night the swearing in ceremony proceeded like any other. We toasted the night with spring water, and he walked to the podium, and that was when it happened. Dead words bristled in his throat. *Friends*, he said, *this week our focus should be on the worlds beyond the mist. Have we lived long enough apart? Is it time to share more widely?* And after the vote was counted unanimous, he called those who would travel beyond, and asked them, one by one, to search out the name of that blossomed tree, for as he said, *I planted one, long ago, with my mother.*

Katelynn E. Carver

The Curio Unbound: Weaving an Intersubjective Tapestry of the Deathless Embodiment of Story

The call to this work, this panel—*We Have Been Pondering The Dead*—was not an ill-suited beckon: for I have, in fact, been pondering death. Dying. What it means to die. The Dead.

But in so doing, I cannot help the niggling voice in the back of my mind that always adds: *and so, as well, The Living.*

I believe that Joan Didion touched on something fundamentally true in stating that "we tell ourselves stories in order to live"[1] —and our stories of life and death are more than just dirges in the making, more than mere inevitability. In looking at the interdisciplinary study of narrative itself, the act of storytelling is revealed as a testament to the fundamental, neuropsychological human need for connection, for the bearing of communal witness to experience with a relational context. In Bettleheim's assertion that in order "to find deeper meaning, one must be able to transcend the narrow confines of a self-centered existence,"[2] we see a evolutionary mind that is built for narrative connections, "addicted," if you will, to the meaning that allows for us to experience life with coherent significance, and that in turn constructs sense from the uncertainty and randomness of our world in order to foster memory, shape personhood, build and alter and mold and grow our very senses of self.[3]

---

1) Joan Didion, *The White Album* (New York: Simon & Schuster, 1979), 11.
2) Bruno Bettelheim, *The Uses of Enchantment: The Meaning and Importance of Fairy Tales* (London: Penguin Books, 1978), 4.
3) Jonathan Gottschall, *The Storytelling Animal: How Stories Make Us Human* (Boston: Houghton Mifflin Harcourt, 2012), 102-103.

And regardless of the context, the process of narrative meaning-making is primarily integration, the product of a dynamic interweaving of the transient with the enduring, the finite with the infinite, the living with the dead until a comingling occurs that is inextricable; a co-creative meaning of what it is to *be* then emerges that eschews the kind of binaries that academic dialogue is so fond of employing: dwelling instead in a liminal miasma of potential that ebbs and flows, gives and takes, and transforms.

As such, while any given human contributing to these stories may wither, may rot, become food for worms: the fact is: they are *food*. They are fodder, grist for a mill that does not cease turning, present within some larger, pseudo-Jungian collective unconscious that situates narrative itself as deathless, as beyond death.

And yet: this is all very broad, very big picture—very forest at the expense of the trees, and we are the trees. We stand, we grow, we shake, we fall: while the forest remains.

But the ground remembers what happened, what once was. And that ground feeds every new tree. The stories bring forth new life. Fairy stories, with the magic of renewal, of resurrection and creation all at once.

Tolkien speaks in one of his greatest essays on the pallor and purpose of the fairy story, and perhaps most memorably, he laments that after a given age, the fairy tale is abandoned as a story—as a source of this fundamental meaning—and lapses instead to the realm of the curio: a curiosity, to be studied with detachment and learned from at a distance, if at all.[4] Tolkien defends the enduring purpose of the fairy story primarily by highlighting its possibilities for an adult reader—as opposed here to a researcher—in creating a Secondary World, a healthy escape that provides comfort, that tends to end happily

4) J.R.R. Tolkien, "On Fairy Stories," in *Tree and Leaf* (New York: Harper Collins, 1964).

where our Primary World doesn't always, and which offers the Great Escape from Death that is impossible beyond the imagined: a "prophylactic against loss," he calls it, a means for the recovery of what once was.

Tolkien further develops this approach from a Christian perspective, but I want to grow this idea from less exclusive soil, and I want to take his "rash adventure" into the World of Faerie, that "perilous land," with "pitfalls for the unwary and dungeons for the overbold"—I want to risk a dungeon for the sake of boldness and say that fairy stories don't stop with age; in fact, they don't take place in other worlds at all. Not at their core. Not where their meaning lies. Their metaphors are not imaginary, not castles in the sky; they are transparent in the right light. They are rooted. They are trees. They are *us*, and they are *ours*.

The *ground*. It *remembers*.

Meménto, homo, quia pulvis es, et in púlverem revertéris

*   *   *

At a given age, the ground meant to be underfoot is used for sitting, the grass meant to cover soil is used for plucking, and the dandelions—oh dear.

I wonder, sometimes, if the ground remembers all of the dandelions sacrificed to a child's curiosity, or boredom, or morbid abandon.

I wonder if there's anger, or there's mourning, somewhere, for their loss, or whether that's what dandelions were made for from the beginning.

Children have strange ways of forming bonds, of discovering alliances that grow into friendships. I played softball as a child, and before each game, we warmed up by playing catch. It was an innocuous, unremarkable home game when I was paired with Maria: a girl with a boy's haircut (it was the nineties, and we were barely five, and gender norms were still fairly prominent in the American Midwest) who was far too distracted by the dandelions in the outfield to remember to move her glove to follow the big-bright-yellow-softball when it was thrown her way.

This led to a bloody lip for Maria and a grudge against me that lasted until she disappeared from the team a few years later, in that way that kids come and go from each other's lives, whispering off into the unknown. As children's stories often are, this tale was short, and I left it behind upon its close.

But Maria had lived behind the school, and you could see her backyard from the playground, and once in a while I would drag my shoes lazily into the dust beneath the swing-set and wonder: about softballs, and bright yellow, and dark red, and dandelions.

The ruts of children's feet beneath a swing are immortal. They never forget.

*   *   *

In *On Fairy Stories*, Tolkien provides a hermeneutic for his own works, shines a light upon what his own publications stand for and provides a lens through which to view the world as a whole. In penning that timeless Oxonian scribble, somewhere between Pembroke Square and *The Bird and Baby*—"In a hole in the ground, there lived a hobbit"[5] — he gives us something that reads more as fairy story than parable. The tendency to relegate such intimations of playful fantasy to the realm of the young, the simple, or the pedestrian is not in itself particularly calamitous: fairy stories lay the foundation for much of cultural narrative.

By its implications, however, this tendency is woefully misguided.

5) J.R.R. Tolkien, *The Hobbit, or, There and Back Again* (Boston: Houghton Mifflin, 1966).

In a global climate of unprecedented change and complexity, to say nothing of pervasive fear messaging, crumbling economies and threats to international security, the "kind of post-traumatic generalized anxiety disorder"[6] currently typifying modern society not only parallels the Great War out of which *The Hobbit* and its successive works were conceived, but also underscores the enduring relevance and significance of its archetypal themes and of story as not merely a human condition, but as a condition of humanity.

In our post-quantum world of infinite complexities, meaning can only be made via integration. In the face of hate, and violence, terrorism, uncertainty, economic decay, catastrophic debt, where the narrative of our experiences should flow with some degree of connectivity, we lean closer to pandemonium: an external disorder that is reflected internally, an inability to structure our experiences and make sense of them. We have to look toward a harmonization of contrasts. We have to seek temperance. We have to find a touchstone in the storm and begin to draw our meaning from the products of the fray.

And this is the purpose of the fairy story. This is the place where what we learn must be marveled at in childhood but *reinforced* across the lifespan. Because if we do not remember our fairy stories, and what they teach, we will forget what it means to find refuge in fantasy in healthy, productive ways; to recognize where escape is necessary and to do it responsibly; to seek consolation and find ways to recover when tragedy strikes so that we might find our footing on even ground, make our way: *make meaning*, once again.

The fairy story teaches us to find balance as we put one foot in front of the other, toward the unknown. This is, indeed, a lesson best learned in childhood: not because

6) John Rutledge & Pamela Rutledge, "The Role for Vigilantes: A Little Duct Tape and Plastic Sheeting and All's Right with the World." *Psychology Today*. Accessed August 18, 2015. https://www.psychologytoday.com/blog/positively-media/201003/the-role-vigilantes-little-duct-tape-and-plastic-sheeting-and-alls.

it should be left there, but because it shapes the way we meet the ground. And the ground, you'll recall: it remembers.

Fairy stories, then, are not merely a foundation, no: they reassert themselves. The perilous realm of Faery is wily, is treacherous, and it tests throughout the life span: *have you forgotten? Did you remember?*

Can you learn again?

*   *   *

Nearly a decade later, a children's story—my children's story—resumed, unbidden: the girl with a boy's haircut now had long curls with bright red highlights that matched my own Matrix RedLights—a big deal for junior high-school in the early aughts. It wasn't this shared sense of style that drew our joint attention to each other, though: it was the book we carried like some people carry the Bible: the compiled single-volume of The Lord of the Rings.

After sizing each other up sufficiently—have you read all of the Histories? Can you speak any Elvish? Which dialect? How well?—Maria and I fell into a quick friendship that expanded both our social circles; her friends became mine, mine became hers, and we were something of the anti-clique: pierced and inked and hair-dyed, with frequent-shopper cards at Hot Topic, who stormed the midnight showings of The Lord of the Rings trilogies in costume and threw Rivendell-themed sweet-sixteens. Through high school, as well as after, we remained the closest of friends. That book, much like the one that brought us together again, found new Tales for the telling, continued on.

It turned out Maria never moved from that house behind the school. One night, we ended up at that playground— now abandoned, for the school had moved onto green pastures and rebuilt elsewhere, the building scheduled for demolition, dust unto dust. But we sprawled across the chain-link bridge, the garish yellow-and-blue plastic recreational equipment of every elementary school from that time, and we stared at the sky, at the stars. Our feet dragged against the pebbles that tore your knees when you stumbled—my own skin long scarred from such encounters, my own blood somewhere on those rocks, and the treads of my shoes long since washed away from beneath the swings, but the force they exerted, the lines they drew: those remained.

The ground; fairy story asked: did we remember?

And we answered: we never forgot.

*   *   *

The older we get, the more the world exerts its own force, creates its own distractions from what we know in our hearts and souls—what we remember from the fairy stories about resilience and recovery and what it means to mourn but then to return—while also causing such mourning and more need for scaffolding to hold to so that we can weather such storms without crumbling, or compromising our selfhoods. Returning to Tolkien's own fairy story, The Hobbit: Bilbo's story, besieged by darkness and doubt as it sometimes is, can be read from a hermeneutical lens of perpetual and recurrent hope—not bereft of hardship and loss, but knowing that life does prevail. And if, as Bilbo says, "where there's life, there's hope," then it is life that typifies the tale. The world of The Hobbit exhibits special concern for experience reshaped and re-envisioned so that the future can be realized in novel ways, can yield deeper meaning, not only despite suffering, but alongside it, co-creative and interwoven to reflect the complexity of experience.

Likewise, in the 2012 film adaptation of The Hobbit, an exchange between the elf queen Galadriel and the wizard Gandalf summarizes the overarching efficacy of the narrative. Galadriel asks: "Why the halfling?" Gandalf's answer is not only moving, but revealing of why Tolkien's tale resonates in an ever-changing world: "I don't know," Gandalf admits. "Saruman believes that it is only great power that can hold evil in check, but that is not what I have found. I have found it is the small things, everyday deeds of ordinary folk that keeps the darkness at bay. Acts of kindness and love. Why Bilbo Baggins? Perhaps it is because I am afraid, and he gives me courage."[7]

And because these events are not dioramas, and because we are the characters: because this is not a curio, Bilbo gives us courage, too. In functioning as more than mere fantasy, in transcending into the realm of formative mythos, *The Hobbit* embodies the Campbellian assertion of the function of mythological archetypes: the assurance that we do not "have to risk the adventure alone, for the heroes of all time have gone before us. The labyrinth is thoroughly known[...]and where we had thought to find an abomination, we shall find a god. And where we had thought to slay another, we shall slay ourselves. Where we had thought to travel outward, we will come to the center of our own existence. And where we had thought to be alone, we shall be with all the world."[8]

Despite these multifaceted boons, the relevance of fantasy is often overlooked, for the very unfounded reasons that Tolkien identifies in *On Fairy Stories*: the tales are put aside, taken for granted, relegated to a time associated with limitations of scope, with fanciful notions that predate maturity, and thus cannot coexist with what it means to be an adult.

And as Gandalf tells Bilbo at the close of the tale: "You are only quite a little fellow in a wide world after all!" To which Bilbo replies: "Thank goodness!"—but we are each of us small creatures, and the immensity of the world can be overwhelming. Like Gandalf's explanation to Galadriel, we, too, are oftentimes afraid.

---

7) *The Hobbit: An Unexpected Journey*, Dir. Peter Jackson. Perf. Ian McKellen, Martin Freeman, Richard Armitage (New Line Cinema, 2012), DVD.
8) Joseph Campbell, *The Hero With A Thousand Faces* (Novato, CA: New World Library, 1949).

Because our myths and stories matter, from the religious significance of parting the Red Sea to the capitalist mythos of the military-industrial complex, from the terrorist narratives of organizations the world over, to the endless, layered chapters of the books lining our shelves: on paper first, and in our lives manifest, our stories matter. So for the sake of Bilbo, for the sake of the story, for the sake of a formative mythos that overcomes its context and speaks to our timeless lived experience and our quintessential human nature; for the sake of a hobbit, we are called to answer the question of "Why the Halfling?" just as Gandalf does: *because he gives us courage.*

*   *   *

It was the last place I ever thought I'd need courage.

Another decade into my own fairy story, I was a bridesmaid in Maria's wedding, her Maid of Honor. The bride herself walked out to Howard Shore's "Concerning Hobbits," and there were lines of Beren and Lúthien meant for the service: even a sign stuck into the ground declaring no admittance unless on "party business." I gifted the bride with a bracelet themed for wizardry; I presented the groom with his very own sword (his new wife, of course, had long since prized her replica of Hadhafang, and it was time they were both armed appropriately).

I was a few margaritas into the open bar—there were six flavors available, and I was dead-set on sampling them all—sipping the very passable raspberry variety, when I passed a vaguely familiar man who was alive with conversation, and overheard him talking of dwarves. I was drawn to him.

It turned out he was vaguely familiar as the brother of one of Maria's friends, one of those subsumed into our larger collective upon meeting and merging social circles; I sat down and swapped my margarita for the perhaps more academic scotch at the table and jumped into the fray, discussing Tolkien at length and lamenting that, for so few degrees of separation between us, this brother of a friend's friend—Christopher, who'd lived and breathed Tolkien his entire life—and I had never truly spoke before. We promised, by the time dawn was coming to the horizon, to remedy this; Facebook, perhaps. I had a conference in a few months in which I was scheduled to discuss the pedagogical merits of The Hobbit, *and I wanted to run a few of the more meticulous allusions by him, if he was willing; he enthusiastically agreed. Tolkien had once again nudged my fairy-story toward progress and newness and embiggenment. All was well.*

Courage, though. Courage.

Christopher died, three months later.

It was unexpected. It was no one's fault. When I hugged his grieving mother at the viewing—barely a stranger, but needing to pay my respects—we talked about how he loved the stories, the lessons in the Tolkien legendarium. He was buried with his well-worn copies, not much younger themselves than his own thirty-some years. In the place of hymns were the film scores and soundtracks. Billy Boyd's final credits track, "The Last Goodbye," was haunting in a way that made the movies, made the novels, the stories immediate: real.

These fairy stories: they persist, yes. But not just in memory, or theory.

Never just *in theory.*

*   *   *

It struck me as I walked to my car in the cold that meeting Maria was where my fairy story began; seeing the book on her desk as it sat upon mine was the play within the play, faery as actor and setting. But this, where a life ends, this was what faery was meant to guard against, the prophylactic, the Great Escape.

It all was tied to the story. Tolkien's story. Christopher's. Maria's. Mine. So *real*. And via the connection, the uncanny way the strands wove together: still touched with enchantment. Still a fairy story, because even if it was not an escape in itself, there was possibility. It wasn't without potential for the new. It was not a curiosity to be studied, static, because the weight I feel anew when I open my own copy of The Fellowship of the Ring is not imaginary. The well-worn pages that accompanied Christopher's body into the ground were not mere curios. They were a part of him. They were parts of ourselves. They were our fairy-stories: or else, we were the pages, the words upon them. Or both, or all.

When the trees in the forest die, new ones maintain the larger forest. The old trees decay and feed the soil, the new trees. The old trees become the pages, in the books, that feed the soul.

They say we can only ponder death in the abstract; I think that's correct. The title of Damien Hirst's shark bathed in formaldehyde is an insight beyond its art: The Physical Impossibility of Death in the Mind of Someone Living. We do not engage death truly as the thing-in-itself. We engage points within a cycle, never ending—because our personal end is beyond the reach of our imagination, beyond the constraints of the self-preservation of an ever-creative and creating human mind. It is beyond our capacity for expression, beyond the reality of physical, embodied, quantifiable death: lack of novelty, the inability to create anew, stagnation. Therefore we ponder death by association, rather than death itself.

In lieu of fully grasping the concept of death, we are left with its mirror: the finite/infinite I AM of Exodus, Descarte's je pense, donc je suis, an answer to the infamous nunnery scene that to BE is the only thing worth the query. We are left with the eisegetical challenge and promise to make newness from death, to carry forth from loss with the story that is synonymous with our endless process of meaning-making, our deathless quest for the wherefore, amidst the endless viscous ephemera, the tohu vabohu that both coalesces and destroys, pure chaos and creative potential as the roots of our being, the very essence of our selves that dance arrhythmic until they stumble upon rhythm.

And if there is more of Gilgamesh to be discovered even now in Kurdistani fragments, if even that epic can continue to grow, we too are invited to evoke what Alice Walker called a sense of "heaven, more a verb than a noun, more a condition than a place [...] all about leading with the heart in whatever broken or ragged state it's in, stumbling forward in faith until, from time to time, we miraculously find our way."[9] And our fairy stories: they are maps to the immortal tale. They recur unexpectedly, unrepentantly, to help us to chart, to understand our world. This is the task of being. This is the meaning-making that Frankl insists we live for,[10] that Richard Rohr identifies as the "life-death-life pattern that always ends in resurrection."[11] I open a book. I smell history on the pages. I see creases I made, there; notes in the margins. I remember when I read it last. I remember how I found it. I think of a wedding, and a softball. I think of Christopher, and the sister, the niece left behind. I think of pages rotting with a corpse beneath the ground. I think of how that means that life can infuse more broadly, can reach greater depths. Make newness, in new ways uncharted before. In need of maps. Fairy stories.

And these? Are so much more than mere curios. *We* are so much more than mere curios.

We are the making of lines in the ground beneath the swings, and we are the swinging. Christopher was the man he lived to be and the story I tell here, and the pages of the book beside a body will become one day the inseparable ground, and we are the ground. We are the memory in the ground. We are the pages.

We are the endless fairy story.

9) Alice Walker, "Alice Walker: After 20 Years, Meditation Still Conquers Inner Space," *The New York Times*, Arts sec.
10) Emily Smith, "A Psychiatrist Who Survived The Holocaust Explains Why Meaningfulness Matters More Than Happiness." *Business Insider.* October 22, 2014. Accessed November 1, 2015. http://www.businessinsider.com/a-lesson-about-happiness-from-a-holocaust-survivor-2014-10.
11) Richard Rohr, "A Message from Fr. Richard Rohr." Center for Action and Contemplation. Accessed September 30, 2015.
https://cac.org/RR-message.

Kendra Leonard

History Faux/Real: the 2006 *Ur-Hamlet*

visit
vimeo.com/album/3749420
for videos

Hamlet is perhaps one of the most often adapted texts by Shakespeare. Even if we consider the word "adaptation" to mean only those performances and productions that vary significantly from the language of the early modern printed sources (rather than every iteration as a standalone adaptation), there are hundreds if not thousands of such approaches to the play. The MIT Global Shakespeares online archive alone hosts dozens of variations of and on *Hamlet*. Yet despite the worldwide embrace of the play, it is one of our most queried, analyzed, studied, broken down, torn apart, re-worked, vex(t)ed texts. Every production—every adaptation—raises new questions. The 2006 *Ur-Hamlet* created by the Danish Nordic Theatre Laboratory/Odin Teatret (DNTL/OT) presents the origins and an adaptation of *Hamlet* in which many aspects of the story of Amleth the Dane are taken off the page and presented through the embodiment of the printed work and codex, music representing the medieval of Asia and Western Europe, and dance.

In the 2006 *Ur-Hamlet*, *Hamlet*/Hamlet/Amleth enters the stage in multiple guises, wherein he is depicted as a book and a man and a character and a ghost and a stereotype, among other things. As the audience sees the multiplicities of Hamlet, the DNTL/OT provides the outline of the action: "On the stage the audience sees the story of a refined royal court glittering from the gold of the Balinese costumes, in which love, intrigues and death are intertwined while Saxo Grammaticus illustrates their story in Latin. All around them, an entire world of immigrants, neglected, excluded, subterranean people move as rats.

They penetrate in silence and lurk in every space left free by the courtiers. But before long this double world in which each group ignores the other is penetrated by plague and contagion."

The goal of the theatre and this production in particular was stated as being to integrate cultural elements of East and West and show the universality of 1. *Hamlet* and 2. oppression of the Other. In an attempt to reverse common stereotypes, the creators designed a show for Western audiences that relocated *Amleth* to a fantasy pan-Asian court comprised of Balinese and Japanese actors and cultural elements. They cast Europeans as the "immigrants" spreading "plague," and Amleth himself as a Brazilian Orxia, alone in the crowds. In doing so the creators called upon various representations of East and West and the medieval through the use of dramatic forms, physical movement, music, and dance. In doing so, they rejected traditional narratives of the medieval as depicted in written documents and testimony and instead sought a fluid reimagining of the past. Although the creators' desire seems to have been a cultural and class-based switch of the too-often historic reality of white European hegemony and its oppression of non-whites, instead the play offers audiences an Indonesian upper class that is corrupt beneath its layers of gold; an Amleth who is played by one of the only black actors to appear and who is dehumanized through his forced play-acting as a dog and through the removal of his voice and its replacement with animalistic bird noises; and a presentation of the medieval East and West as, respectively, the epitome of louche savagery and the height of sophistication for their times. In trying to discard the hegemonies of the past as described in literature, the creators nonetheless reinscribed inequality and bias in an unwritten form.

The play uses the music of former British colonies and faux-medieval music that mimics Northern European liturgical music in addition to a number of musical pieces from and musical references to Asia, particularly the gamelan of Indonesia. This soundscape is intended to be part of "an exchange of cultural manifestations" that suggests the view of Shakespeare from outside of the Anglophone world. The production was designed to bring together different acting traditions from across the world; in doing so, it also incorporated music from these cultures. The *Ur-Hamlet* uses Asian musics played by Asian and Western instruments to suggest the complexities of the story and employs faux-Northern European medieval music to emphasize its age, history, and origins. This music surrounds the Hamlet role and makes him both a "medieval" and "other" character; in addition, the citational musical environment of the play reifies and negates stereotypes of the medieval and its relevance in Shakespeare's work. It emphasizes the chronological distance between the present and the early modern, but draws the early modern back even further by suggesting that the story of Amleth as told by Saxo went unchanged and undeveloped through Shakespeare to the present. It asks audiences to equate the medieval with the early modern and to regard both as so distant as to be completely Other. At the same time, it offers a view that the Amleth story contains chronological and geographical universals, and that the setting is malleable or even irrelevant.

The DNTL/OT production begins with a long recitation of a portion of Saxo Grammaticus's *Amleth, Prince of Denmark,* first in Latin and then in English. In the 2006 performances, Saxo is played by a white woman wearing long robes and a baldpate, both of which signify "monk" in popular culture. Indeed, the first page of the script reads, "THE MONK SAXO DIGS INTO THE DARK AGE . . .," digging up bones, signifiers of the distant past.[1] The performance space is lit by torches and oil lamps, and the music is that of an Indonesian gamelan ensemble, which uses pitched percussion that is struck with mallets. Already the production, as part of formally setting the action, conjures up a popular "dark" view of the period and establishes it as foreign and exotic and barbaric. This concept, at least for white European audiences, is emphasized by the music that immediately follows.

1) Ur-Hamlet Scenario, 1. http://www.odinteatretarchives.com/ close-up/media/ur-hamlet/documents/2006_Scenario.pdf

Saxo's entrance is heralded by what the scenario calls a "butoh flute," likely a shakuhachi, or traditional Japanese bamboo flute. As Saxo raises up Prince Amleth's skull, a flashback showing King Horwendill (Old Hamlet)'s murder is played out through Balinese dance, accompanied by traditional gambuh gamelan (tuned percussion) music. (See video 1: Horwendill murder.) Vicious action is thus paired with medieval music from the East. Saxo—a Westerner—recounts this story for the audience in terms of a more primitive society; he himself is at a remove from it in his European monastery. This establishes two things: that Saxo's story has been transplanted into a fictional world cobbled together using various distinct elements of different national and ethnic arts practices from the East; and that Saxo's medievalism, as "dark" as it will be shown, is yet superior to that of the Other culture in question. Ultimately, with his scholasticism and the longevity of the written word, Saxo will outlast everyone. The use of authentic medieval music from Asia is in direct contrast with newly-created medieval-sounding music for Europe. The message this musicking brings is unclear: is Asian music required to be authentic because it is being appropriated here by white creators, albeit while being performed by Asian artists? Is it meant to suggest that all human origins are the same? Does it argue that the past of Asia is somehow more real or better preserved that than of the West, for which simulacra is appropriate? Are audiences to hear the production's faux-medieval music as a signifier of the widespread construction of the medieval period by non-specialists?

The horrors of the Western medieval world are visited only on the court after further immorality has taken place: Feng has married Geruta, and Amleth has had sex with his foster-sister. At the wedding feast of two "plague rats," a Noh actor appears as a priest, chanting and swinging a censor. His faux-medieval chant refocuses the audience's attention to the chronological setting, and, as guests begin falling ill of the plague, its own hazards. (See video 2: Wedding.) Likewise, the period is further coded as one of chaos, disease, and political infiltration when the women of the European "plague rats" join together in a Macedonia song with roots in distant history. Accompanied by Western brass instruments and drums, they lead an assault on the Asians in whose court they live. This communally performed music, with all voices together, suggests the rats' greater abilities in self-governance, organization, and the perpetuation of a culture. (See video 3: Rat Song.) Does the use of ancient folk song here represent a non-elite authenticity of culture that is placed in opposition with the elite music of Western monasteries, which is represented by musical simulacra? Or do the creators employ the folk song because it resonates with the concept that some elements of culture survive over time because of their appeal to and performance by broader socio-economic spectra of peoples? If this song and the gamelan music are actual medieval works, then why is the medieval West assigned new music?

In contrast, when Amleth returns from killing Feng to establish his new rule, Balinese dancing and music is used to represent drunkenness and lack of cognitive abilities among the dissipated court members. Amleth, his movements drawn from candomblé, defeats them easily. Yet Amleth's vocality is compromised from the start. The creators take Saxo's story of the prince crowing like a cock to perform madness and instill it as the voice of Amleth throughout. Even at the end of the play, when he is asked to announce his new world rules for order, Amleth can only scream to each compass point while another actor sings the rules. The voices and figures of both are gradually engulfed by Balinese music and dance, and the establishment of a child king, in Balinese dress, suggests that European and New World enlightenment have done nothing to elevate the barbarity of the imagined pan-Asian court. Amleth dances a *baris*, a Balinese war dance, further suggesting the court's violent and uncivilized nature.

Ultimately what we find in *Ur-Hamlet* are different kinds of variously real and fake medieval music used to portray the fake medieval in multiple, equally constructed and mediated cultures. I'm not arguing that productions should use "authentic" music; I'm not even suggesting that there is such thing as authenticity, not any more than there is a single text for *Hamlet*. What does all of this fake medieval music really say about the *Ur-Hamlet* and how does that affect its messages about social issues in the European Union, historic and current racial and class-based inequities, and diversity?

1.   It suggests that some medieval musical (and other) cultures were homogenous. Chant, as depicted here, represents all of medieval music and the music of culture in a white, male-dominated society. Traditional Balinese music, likewise, stands in for all medieval Indonesian (and most South Asian) musical culture. Amleth by himself is accompanied by Brazilian candomblé music. This is all too easily reduced to (chronologically from the beginning of the production):

white medieval people are to chant as Asian medieval people are to gamelan as black medieval people are to candomblé.

Which leads me to think:

2.   It reinforces – mostly – connections between elite status and music. Chant developed and was brought forth in the flourishing of the Catholic Church, and enormously wealthy institution. It was also the preserve of the educated and literate, and of families who gave children to monasteries and convents. In Java, gamelan ensembles dating from the 8th century are associated with royalty – as we see in *Ur-Hamlet* – and wealthy temples. The instruments themselves were made from precious metals, rare woods, and other valuable materials. Even candomblé, which grew out of African beliefs brought to Brazil with enslaved laborers, has become a solidly middle-class religion, practiced by both Afro-Brazilians and whites. One could argue that this music is suitable for *Amleth* because it does take place at court, but the "plague rats" are musically signified by vernacular song, not chant or gamelan.

3.   It confirms that for most people, the medieval as a whole—elite music notwithstanding—was a "dark age." By framing the Indonesian setting of the story

of Amleth with the narration of the white, educated, literate Saxo, the creators default to presenting the story and its Asian characters, their culture, and their music as Other. It is foreign, exotic, and, as the inclusion of the *baris* dance shows, violent and coarse. The musicians playing modern western instruments are on a raised platform and well-lit and amped, and the singers performing chant and chant-like materials have mics. The gamelan and Brazilian music performers are on the ground, less well-lit, and their music is not provided with clarifying or broadcasting technology. The music of the West is literally illuminated above that of the East. Furthermore, most of the production is lit by torchlight: in such a visual atmosphere, what is most visible? Saxo's gleaming white head. Indeed, it is difficult to make out the faces of the Balinese court and Amleth—even the white, European "plague rats" are more literally visible.

My reading of this piece is that it reifies positions of white privilege and Eurocentrism. Erik Exe Christofferson notes that much of the group's work deals with "'foreignness' as a fundamental condition in the twentieth and twenty-first centuries."[2] In their *Ur-Hamlet*, the idea of the medieval as foreign is present both in the plot and metadiegetically in the production. The program for the production notes that, "Diversity is the basic matter of theatre," but the overall citational environment of cultures and music is one in which the medieval achievements of white Europeans are more equal than that of Others.

2) Christofferson, Erik Exe. 2008. "Theaturm Mundi: Odin Teatret's Ur-Hamlet." New Theatre Quarterly 24 (2): 107–25.

About the Authors

Greg Allendorf is originally from Cincinnati, OH. He holds graduate degrees from The University of Cincinnati and Purdue University. His poems have appeared in such journals as *Smartish Pace*, *Subtropics*, and *The Portland Review*. He currently lives in Columbia, MO, where he is a third-year PhD candidate and Creative Writing Fellow at The University of Missouri-Columbia.

Jonathan Basile is a fiction writer, philosopher, and computer programmer. He has created an online universal library, libraryofbabel.info, and an online universal image archive. He has written about the project in *The Paris Review Daily*, *Nexos*, and *Flavorwire*. His work has been exhibited at Recess Art and Good Work Gallery.

Paula Billups is an artist and writer whose works and curriculum vitae can be found on her websites at www.paulabillups.com and www.dragonfoodpress.com. Her blog is paulabillupsart.blogspot.com and her Facebook page is under Paula Billups Artist as well as Facebook.com/babel.librarian.

Born in South Carolina, raised in Northeast Ohio, shaped by Boston, and currently settled—and reveling—in Fife, **Katelynn E. Carver** is a postgraduate researcher in Theology, Imagination, and the Arts at the University of St Andrews, where she is currently pursuing interdisciplinary work in postsecular, process-oriented theopoetics. She earned her B.A. and B.S. from Baldwin Wallace University in Ohio, her MTS from Harvard University in Massachusetts, and she is currently a PhD candidate in Scotland. A Marvel Comics enthusiast, a firm believer in the Oxford Comma, and a painter when she can get her hands on a good set of oils: if Katelynn's awake, she's probably writing, or reading, or watching the ebb and flow of the tides on the North Sea with a cup of tea in hand.

Alison Fraser is the author of *Animalia*.

Eileen G'Sell's cultural criticism and poetry can be found in *Salon, Flavorpill, The Rumpus, Playspace, Boston Review, DIAGRAM, Conduit,* and the *Denver Quarterly,* among others. Her book *Portrait of My Ex with Giant Burrito* is available from BOAAT Press. She currently teaches rhetoric and film at Washington University, and hip-hop poetry through the Hip-Hop Chess Federation. She lives in St. Louis and New York.

Les Kay is the author of the full-length poetry collection *Home Front* (Sundress Publications, forthcoming 2017) as well as the chapbooks *Badass* (Lucky Bastard Press, 2015) and *The Bureau* (Sundress Publications, 2015). He is also a co-author of the collaborative poetry chapbook *Heart Radicals* (ELJ Publications, forthcoming 2016). His fiction is forthcoming in *Hermeneutic Chaos,* and his poems have been published in journals such as *Borderlands: Texas Poetry Review, The McNeese Review, PANK, Redactions, Whiskey Island,* and *The White Review.* Follow him here: www.leskay.com.

Michael Kelleher is the author of the poetry collection *Visible Instruments,* forthcoming from Chax Press as well as the collections *Human Scale* and *To Be Sung,* both from BlazeVOX. From 2008-2013 he produced *Aimless Reading,* a blog project in which he photographed, catalogued, and wrote about the more than 1200 titles in his library. He is the Director of the Windham-Campbell Literature Prizes at Yale University and the former Artistic and Associate Director of Just Buffalo Literary Center in Buffalo, NY.

Kendra Preston Leonard is a musicologist and music theorist whose work focuses on music and stage and screen history, particularly music and adaptations of Shakespeare; and women and music in the twentieth and twenty-first centuries. Her work has appeared in *The Oxford Handbook of Music and Disability Studies, Gender and Song in Early Modern England, This Rough Magic, Upstart Crow, Early Modern Studies Journal, The Journal of Historical Biography, The Journal of Musicological Research,* and *Current Musicology,* among other journals and collections. She is the author of *Shakespeare, Madness and Music: Scoring Insanity in Cinematic Adaptations*, and is currently at work on a project examining the musical depiction of the early modern period in film.

Matt McBride lives in Wuhan, China, where he works as a visiting professor of English at Huazhong Agricultural University. His poetry has appeared in or is forthcoming from *Another Chicago Magazine, Cream City Review, FENCE, Juked, The Mississippi Review, Ninth Letter,* and *PANK* amongst others. His chapbook, *Cities Lit by the Light Caught in Photographs* was published by H_NGMN_N books in 2012.

Mike Rose-Steel has published four collaborative collections of poetry and is the founding editor for Spindlebox Press. Alongside text-art projects with the Exegesis group, he is completing a PhD in Wittgenstein and poetics at the University of Exeter, UK. His inspiration largely comes from philosophical or formal puzzles, and the Cornish environment, which is wet.

Thea Tomaini is Associate Professor of English (Teaching) at the University of Southern California Department of English. Her field of study is the Early Modern period. She is the author of *Sworn Bond in Tudor England*, NC: McFarland Press, 2011. She has also published articles on ghost legends and death fascination of the sixteenth and seventeenth centuries. Her current academic projects include a book entitled *The Corpse As Text: Death Fascination and Cultural Ideals in England 1700-1900* (forthcoming from Boydell Publishing), and she is also editor of a collaborative volume entitled *Dealing With The Dead In The Middle Ages* (forthcoming from Brill Publishing). She is on the executive board of MEARCSTAPA, an academic society dedicated to the study of monsters and the supernatural. In 2015 she became Co-Editor of *Preternature*, an academic journal dedicated to the study of the supernatural. Professor Tomaini also publishes poetry. She has published individual poems in various poetry journals, and her current writing project is a book of poetry entitled *Everyday Ghosts*. She has yet to see a ghost.

Angela Warner recently finished her MA in Medieval Studies from the University of Toronto 13 years after starting it. She is currently an Independent Scholar in the midst of co-authoring an edition of Middle French Prayers and working on fellowship and PhD applications. She is certain her PhD will take less time to complete than her MA. Her first chapbook, *Weaving Spirit* (LyricalMyrical Press), came out in 2013, and you can find her essays and occasionally her poetry on her website, http://noeticnuance.com. Her 2015 NaPoWriMo poetry was found only on Twitter, though, because she needed a different sort of challenge.

Ruth Williams is the author of *Conveyance* (Dancing Girl Press, 2012). Her poetry has appeared in *Michigan Quarterly Review*, *jubilat*, *Sou'wester*, and *Third Coast* among others. Currently, she is an Assistant Professor of English at William Jewell College.

Tracy Zeman's poems have appeared in *Beloit Poetry Journal*, *jubilat*, *The Sonora Review*, *TYPO*, and other journals. Her manuscript *Empire of Grass* has recently been a finalist in numerous contests. Tracy is the Poetry Editor at *Quiddity: An International Literary Journal*, and she works at Illinois Audubon Society, a conservation organization founded in 1897. She lives in Springfield, IL, with her husband and daughter.

www.ingramcontent.com/pod-product-compliance
Lightning Source LLC
Chambersburg PA
CBHW071237090426
42736CB00014B/3115